Following the Sandhill Cranes in Colorado

ENTICED INTO BIRDING

From the Journals of Evelyn Horn

For Mel,
Enjoy My Birds ?
Evey Horn

WESTERN REFLECTIONS PUBLISHING COMPANY®
Montrose, CO

ISBN 1-932738-05-3

Library of Congress Control Number: 2004108725

Cover drawing of Cranes by Sally Dearmond

Cover and text design: Laurie Goralka Design

First Edition
Printed in the United States of America

Western Reflections Publishing Company®
219 Main Street
Montrose, CO 81401
www.westernreflectionspub.com

this book is dedicated to

Allen Horn

ACKNOWLEDGMENTS

The author is responsible for any errors that occur within the text. I thank the Vela family for their help and concern over these years. I also wish to thank Allen Horn, Lillian Minor, David Galinat, and Karen Derrick for their suggestions during the preparation of the manuscript. And my thanks to Melvin Peterson for sharing his knowledge of the Hart's Basin Cranes and again to David Galinat for the expertise in bird identification that he has so kindly shared with me. I also wish to thank David Chism: Without his assistance in "things computer," this little book could never have become a reality.

Crane Drawings by Sally Dearmond

NOTE: Bird names are from *The Sibley Guide to Birds* by Sibley, David Allen.
Plant names are from *A Utah Flora* by Welsh, S. L., Atwood, N. D., Goodrich, S., Higgins, L. C.

HART'S BASIN OR FRUITGROWERS RESERVOIR

THE HAPPY CIRCUMSTANCE:
THE BIRDS FOUND THE WATER
AND THE BIRDERS FOUND THE BIRDS

Hart's Basin, or Fruitgrowers Reservoir, is now designated as an IBA (Important Bird Area). But it is neither a wildlife refuge nor a bird sanctuary. Rather, it is an irrigation reservoir created by the orchardists, farmers, and ranchers of the immediate area.

As the water is drawn out for irrigation each season, the resulting mud-flat is often a shorebird heaven. When it's frozen in the winter, it's sometimes a Bald Eagle playground.

The land beneath the water and to the high-water mark is the property of the Bureau of Reclamation and is thus public. But I've observed that people walking here are disturbing to the birds. By far, the best blind is your car, parked on North Road (known for years as "N Road"). North Road crosses the reservoir (the "causeway" in my writings) and is a main thoroughfare. We humans have many other places in which to play: It's my sincerest hope that this one small area will be left for the birds.

All of the land surrounding the reservoir is private, not public. Please, be courteous. Pull off the road before you stop. Please use only your side of the road. Please, be courteous to the birds, too. And may we maintain our "happy circumstance."

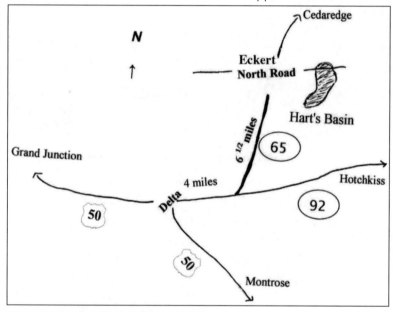

DIRECTIONS TO HART'S BASIN

1) From Delta, take Highway 92 toward Hotchkiss. Drive four (4) miles.

2) Turn left onto Highway 65 to Cedaredge and Grand Mesa. Go about 6 miles to the intersection of Highway 65 and North Road (or N Road). Note: landmark on your left is the

stonework Presbyterian Church and the Big E Country Store is on your right.

3) Turn right (or east) onto North Road.

4) Go about half a mile and you will reach the top of a hill (Crane Point to this writer) that overlooks Fruitgrowers Reservoir or Hart's Basin. This is the setting for much of this book.

PLEASE NOTE: This road has been known as "N Road" for years but now is to be called North Road. The new signs may or may not be up.

CONTENTS

Cranes' Spring

FIRST BIG FLOCK 2
SANDHILL MORNING 5
WHOOPER 9
WHITE DOES NOT A WHOOPER MAKE 12
BUFFLEHEAD 15
CANADA GOOSE 18
APRIL FOOL'S 1997 21

Early Summer

EARED GREBE 26
AMERICAN AVOCET 29
BLACK-NECKED STILT 32
WILSON'S PHALAROPE 34
KILLDEER 37
RED-WINGED BLACKBIRD 40

High Summer

GREAT EGRET 44
SWALLOWS 47
MALLARD 50
AMERICAN PIPIT 53
AMERICAN WHITE PELICAN 57
SORA 59
WESTERN GREBE 62

Autumn

GREAT BLUE HERON 68

STELLER'S JAY 71

DIPPER 74

EASTERN BLUE JAY 77

MAGPIE 79

Along the Migration Route

MIGRATION ROUTE 82

WILSON'S WARBLER 85

COMMON NIGHTHAWK 88

COCHETOPA PASS 92

SAY'S PHOEBE 97

SAGUACHE 101

RIFT VALLEY: THE SAN LUIS .103

GREASEWOOD-FLAT PELICANS 107

DROUGHT AND BLACK-CROWNED NIGHT-HERONS . . .110

MONTE VISTA REFUGE: AVOCETS 114

BOSQUE DEL APACHE: FLY-OUT 117

BOSQUE DEL APACHE: FLY-IN 119

Winter Time

NORTHERN HARRIER 122

EAGLE ON ICE 124

AMERICAN KESTREL 127

COMMON MERGANSER 130

EURASIAN WIGEON 133

It's Spring Again

FIRST LIGHT 136
LEWIS'S WOODPECKER 138
RAVEN 141
HOODED MERGANSER 144
SEPT. 2002 HART'S BASIN WHOOPERS ARE GONE . . .146
"NONE OTHERWISE THAN CRANES" 149

APPENDIX A
Cranes of the World

WHAT'S SO SPECIAL ABOUT CRANES? 154
CRANES OF THE WESTERN HEMISPHERE
        MIGRATORY SANDHILL POPULATIONS 156
WHOOPING CRANE 163
CRANES OF THE WORLD: AFRICA 168
EURASIAN CRANES OF BROAD DISTRIBUTION 175
ONE ANSWER GETS YOU TEN 179
WHO'S WHO AND WHO'S WHERE 182
CRANES OF THE WORLD 184
EPILOG: WHOOPING CRANE MARCH 2004 186

BIBLIOGRAPHY 188

INDEX 191

Dear Reader,

I invite you into my mind,
that you might see through my eyes.

Cranes'

Spring

First Big Flock

Out the back door...Meadowlark's song. Cool breeze...glad that I have on my coat and stocking cap. Silhouettes of barren trees line the top of Antelope Hill. The predawn sky is a study of gray on gray with a few high, thin clouds. Last night there were over 400 Cranes at Hart's Basin but there's not a single call in this morning's chill air. The steering wheel's cold to the touch...nice to have gloves. Down the dirt road toward the reservoir...no Cranes in Vela's fields...a flock of Magpies in a tree...a wheel of Starlings over the pasture. Drive up the hill and out onto Crane Point.

Set up the spotting scope...not a Crane in Vela's fields. Scan over to the Hart's Basin spread...looks gray along the northwest pond. I can see a few Cranes along the edge....WOW! All that gray is actually Sandhill Cranes! Down for a better look. Most are quiet...many are standing on one leg. Several Canada Geese squawk and take off as I stop the car but only a few of the Cranes even look at me. Trying to estimate their number is a matter of counting gray humps...most heads are tucked under wing...the sentry bird keeps a wary eye but it seems that I'm non-threatening.

Going left to right...10...20...a 100 Cranes. Now 110...190. Wait...already counted those. Start again...110...160...200...300...400...460...470 for a total. Try again, this time going from right to left. They're beginning to move around...wish they'd be still. A 100...130...200. Something has disturbed the flock of Pintails on the pond...back to the Cranes...350...360. My birds are becoming active...stretching, preening, walking about. A few are in that pre-flight

stance...necks stretched out, standing on tiptoe. And they fly...above my car...across the road to Vela's field. My window of "count time"
is over. Sun's nearly up. More Cranes fly by.

A car shatters the silence...speeds by...the birds go about their bird business. Must be 30 colorful Green-winged Teal foraging along the water's edge...a pair of gray-brown Gadwall...Mallards. Ah! Here's a pair of solid red-colored Cinnamon Teal, the first I've been sure of this season...things begin to look blurred...another pair of Teal emerges from the dried cattails. Now I have "ghost ducks" swimming in the rising mist. A Pintail taking a bath...brrrr! It's hard to tell where the water ends and the fog begins. I'll save this scene in my memory file for some fretful future day.

On down to the northeast ponds. There's a raptor in an inlet tree...a sleeping Red-tailed Hawk. White-bodied Mergansers are abundant out on the reservoir...a small group of Redheads. The tawny marsh grass is strewn with poet's diamonds, droplets of frozen dew. The hummocks of dried tules glisten with frost where there is shadow...only to grow dull and plain in the sun's low rays.

Scan further out...Black-white ducks... Goldeneyes. A disturbance way out toward the middle...Northern Shovelers swimming in circles to stir up food for breakfast. I can clearly hear the noisy Cranes half a mile away but now I'm busy with other birds. The mist dissipates but the water's surface shimmers with the temperature change... looks like a desert mirage. Since I can't see much, I'll just listen. A gentle chirping duck sound...Pintail? The raucous quack of a female Mallard...the soft, reedy call of her mate. Wings overhead...Great Blue Heron. For several years I've experienced this sort of morning with each "first-big-flock" of Sandhills. And each season these moments grow more precious.

SANDHILL MORNING

Sun's bright and there's a gentle breeze. The Sandhill Cranes are scattered all across Vela's ranch...about 200 along the near shore...more than a 100 between the outbuildings and the trees to the southwest that edge the dam area. More than 300 in the pasture right below us keeping company with the cows and their calves. One of the frisky calves decides to investigate a foraging Crane...the bird looks at him...the calf bounces forward...and the Crane walks stiff legged toward the calf. But discretion is the better part of valor and the calf returns to the safety of mother's side. The Sandhill, at nearly 4-feet-tall, stands about as high as the calf. With wings out-spread the bird is close to 6-feet-wide. Formidable.

Below us, I see a car stopping near the old cottonwood along the country road edging the field with its Cranes. People get out and look...the birds are wary but they don't fly. I remember our first

spring when Allen and I walked that road and, at take-off, the Cranes flew right over us as we stood in awe. Then, the Cranes appeared to be all legs and neck, dressed in a uniform gray. But later a better pair of binoculars revealed the legs to be black with long toes. The bills were long and sharply pointed...the birds dug deep into the ground and flipped cow pies with ease. I realized that such a bill could clearly become a weapon.

Now as I walk up to my spotting scope (set it up earlier this morning) I remember the amazement of first seeing the red crown on top of the head, of the shades of gray, and the occasional rusty wash along the breast and sides, and wondering about it all. Now I watch closely and I can see that some of my birds seem to stay together. I know now that three is the magic number: a mated pair and their young one from last spring, and that when they fly they will try to remain together.

A gentleman asks to view through the scope (be my guest). And I reminisce about myself and the Sandhill Cranes. Local folks have come here to this hilltop for years to view the evening arrival and morning take-off of Cranes. Allen and I are Johnny-come-lately, for we came here in 1989. We'd been through the area for years on our way from Las Vegas, Nevada, to Denver to visit our families, but our trips were in August. Though I didn't disbelieve that there might be birds at Hart's Basin (shown as Fruitgrowers Reservoir on the map), I never really accepted the reports of hundreds, even thousands of Sandhill Cranes. After all, when we saw the reservoir in August it was just a dried mud-flat.

We chose to stay for a winter in Eckert (to see if I could tolerate the cold weather, after thirty years in Las Vegas, Nevada), so we rented a house about half a mile from Hart's

Basin. The water kept flowing down Alfalfa Ditch and into the reservoir until the main portion was full. There was even water in the marshland area on the north side of North Road, which crosses the reservoir. Since there was water on both sides, I dubbed it "the causeway."

And then the Cranes came. A few in early March, warbling on high and spiraling down to the fields and shoreline: I was mesmerized. But by mid-March the birds were coming nearly every evening, and each day the flocks seemed to increase. They would be out of sight overhead and I would wonder, "Are my ears deceiving me and is my imagination running wild?" But then tiny black specks appeared. Sometimes they flew on, but other times they began a spiral downward, growing larger and larger until they became great gray birds. Lower and lower as they called in answer, it seemed, to those on the ground. Then the legs and feet came down as landing gear, the tips of the great wings cupped, and the birds paraglided down to land in the midst of the flock. A couple of running steps, fluff the feathers, and begin to hunt for food: the proverbial "piece of cake." But now I know that they likely flew, in this one day, from the San Luis Valley to cross over North Pass near Gunnison at 10,000 feet altitude.

And now a morning such as this. Carol Vela called earlier to invite me down to the ranch to see the Cranes through her sliding glass doors. They were in the field just across the driveway. Sandhills, close up and personal! And now standing here at Crane Point, the ground has warmed to provide thermal updrafts, and take-off draws near. It's 9:30. Some of the Cranes grow restless, even though others seem content to continue their foraging or preening or whatever. Finally a few stretch out their necks, walk on "tip-toe," run a few steps and are airborne. Others follow in groups of three or twenty or a hundred. They must gain altitude to continue their northward journey, and so the birds circle and circle, gaining a bit with each turn. But since they started at different times, their spirals are all at different levels. The birds "talk" incessantly and the din is overwhelming. And once again I stand in the shadow of the Cranes. Finally they become smaller and smaller against the blue sky and then they "V-out" as they prepare to fly over Grand Mesa at 10,000 feet.

When they are gone, the silence is overwhelming.

Betty Davis and I chat with Helen and Mike Ayers about the great excitement and pleasure of these mornings. We note this morning's count, both birds and people, and commend our good fortune of living in this special little spot by this overlooked irrigation reservoir with its spring migration of Sandhill Cranes.

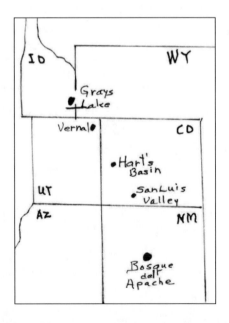

Migration Route
of the Rocky
Mountain
Population

WHOOPER

The truck bounces along across the stubble of the alfalfa field. The Sandhill Cranes look up at us, walk a few leisurely steps away, and then continue to forage. Over the years, they've become used to Jimmy Vela and his silage truck so that on this spring morning we're just part of their accepted landscape.

And gradually we draw closer to the Great-White-Bird...the Whooping Crane who has traveled with this flock for several years.

Nearly 5-feet-tall and shining white...a real standout among the context of the gray-on-gray of the Sandhills. The cattle are following closely now, assured of warm, moist corn-silage, and as Jimmy releases his precious cargo, the cattle set to the serious business of breakfast. The birds watch. In my mind's eye I see the winter browns of the fallow fields and then the harrow turning it into row upon row of dull-brown-shiny-brown. Then comes the planting, and I hope for gentle rains. Early summer and the irrigation pipes lie stark white against the tender greens of new growth, and the Brewer's Blackbirds walk among the few cows that are left at the ranch after the main herd has gone to the high country for a summer of leisurely grazing. And finally, late summer, with the harvesting machinery, and truck load after truck load make the trips from fields to the silage pit by Crane Point. And this truck carries some of that work's culmination: winter feed for the herd.

Though there's plenty to eat right under their noses, the cattle continue to slowly follow the silage truck, apparently preferring the warmest possible breakfast. And the Cranes move in behind them, gleaning the fragrant silage. The Whooper eats a bit too, and then moves toward the pond. Jimmy drives this old truck across the bird's path and now we're within only a few feet of this magnificent Whooper. Allen is busy with the camera and I'm glued to my binoculars. To see, up so very close, the features that I've marveled at through the spotting scope from the top of the hill, a good quarter mile away. The brilliance of the red crown, the blackness of the facial pattern, the black, leathery legs, and the intelligence in the red-orange eye as the bird observes us. And Jimmy comes to a halt. The bird gazes at us, walks on toward the pond (clearly a drink is more important than our possible threat).

But the Whooper decides that the reservoir's water will be better and he makes his way toward the shore, giving us a grandstand view of his stately gait. Clunk-clunk-rattle-rattle and Jimmy quietly drives the truck behind the Whooper and his accompanying Sandhills. They seem oblivious of us...what a handy blind is a vehicle! Now heads down, scoop the water, heads up and up and up...swallow. A Sandhill's neck, at 23-inches, is shorter than that of the larger Whooper, but it's a long way to pour down a bit of water. And I think of their windpipes or tracheas: for the Sandhill's is about 48-inches-long and the Whooper's is nearly 5-feet-long. How do they keep all that in a neck that is shorter than the trachea? The trachea is made up of tough cartilaginous rings that keep it from collapsing or binding. The extra length lies in convoluted loops in the chest, along the sternum under the wing muscles: think of the folded curves of a French horn.

Now the Whooper preens and stretches...about 7-foot wingspan of shimmering white with black wing tips. Spectacular! But our kind guide has many other jobs to complete this morning. And although the Vela family makes time for these migrating Cranes each spring, this is a working ranch. So we return across the field with its contented cows and foraging Cranes. Within a couple of hours the ground will warm sufficiently and these birds will ride the thermal updrafts to attain altitude and continue their migration to the nesting grounds to the north. By that moment, I'll be back up on Crane Point to stand in awe as they spiral, spiral upwards and, among the gray Sandhills, my Whooping Crane will show his greater size and brilliant white plumage even more than he does here on the ground. How fortunate am I.

WHITE DOES NOT A WHOOPER MAKE

A MARCH EVENING

This is a fair sized group of Sandhill Cranes...I'd guess about 500. Wind's up...looks like the predicted storm is about to arrive. Had a phone call about a possible Whooping Crane and here it is, foraging along the ditch to the left of the pasture cottonwood...all I can see is its back. Set up the spotting scope so I'll be ready to watch when I get a chance. The Cranes are often restless when they arrive and such is the case this evening. Lots of vocalization and preening. Some are flipping over the cow pies looking for insects. Others are down at the water, drinking and bathing. Now the white bird raises its head...focus the spotting scope... there's the red crown...but the black facial "crescent" is missing. It's NOT a Whooper. Head's down again...darn! Up again and I can see the plumage on the neck is gray instead of white. It's a Sandhill from the neck up! The bird steps out of the ditch, walking along with the other Sandhills...same size rather than larger, as is a Whooper.

Whooper

Sandhill

And the feathers have a yellowish cast...sort of ivory instead of shining white. So it's not a Whooping Crane. Wonder if it's the hybrid...but there are no leg bands visible at all. Some of the folks say that there are more Sandhills down in the northwest pond...swing the scope around and, sure enough, there are as many along the pond down there as we have here in the pasture at the base of Crane Point.

Down to the causeway to check it out. Easily another 500 Cranes here...along the edges of the pond and back in the dried cattails. Plenty of other waterfowl, too, and I can hear a Marsh Wren. Two Golden Eagles perched in the inlet trees. I'll return early tomorrow morning when the birds are quiet and I'll get a more accurate count then.

THREE DAYS LATER

Just back from Grand Junction and our neighbor, Dave Bennison, stopped to tell me about another possible Whooper at Hart's Basin. Hurry down to see and half a dozen folks concur: It's a Whooper! But the bird is in the shoreline brush and difficult to see...looks white...and large. But I'm hesitant since the Whoopers usually stop here late in the season, and this is only March. Set up the spotting scope so that I can focus quickly when I get a chance. There are only three of these endangered birds left from the experiment of the 1980s, and the possibility of a Whooper really gets the adrenaline flowing! Walking this way...now turning toward the water...the back is grayish, not shining white. Then moving through the tamarisk with half a dozen Sandhills...now along the pasture's edge...same size as the others. Now I can see the red crown on its head...a yellow band on the right leg...nothing visible on the left leg. Magnification up...can't read the numbers. But this bird lacks the black facial crescent that's the hallmark of the Whooping Crane. So...an albino? Reportedly there are three or four. Or is this the one and only hybrid? Hope to gather more adequate information in the future...I'd sure like to know who's who!

The West Elk Mountains gleam white with snow, a Red-tailed Hawk soars between us and the Grand Mesa. The wakes of a dozen waterfowl streak the calm surface of the reservoir. The cows graze in the alfalfa while their calves romp in the twilight. And the pasture below Crane Point is filled with great gray birds. A special place to be on this March evening.

BUFFLEHEAD

The day started cool and cloudy. Last night's Cranes had to work hard to gain sufficient altitude to leave this morning. Now the evening sky is clear and at least 500 new Cranes have arrived. Out on the water are lots of white birds, Gulls and Western Grebes, while a week ago the only white ones were Common Mergansers. This wetland stage is changing swiftly now. Hundreds of Canada Geese, Ring-necked Ducks, Green-winged Teals, and Mallards were here, now only a few remain. Hope that some stay for the breeding season. Don't see the two immature Golden Eagles. Wonder if they will become a pair. I count six Great Blue Herons, and over a hundred Coots, stubby little birds, all black with white beaks. Their arrival always amazes me...can't imagine them flying during migration. Getting from one puddle to the next seems to be a big job, but here they are.

THROUGH THE SPOTTING SCOPE

Looking back along the shore from the causeway, I can see the Cranes milling about...several out in the shallows preening and bathing. And there's another "which-is-it-duck." It's bright white on the top of its head...brilliant green streak from the eye to the back of its head...American Wigeon? I recall that at first I just looked at the Cranes, but now I keep seeing other birds. Never dreamed that a spotting scope could lead me into such fascinating terrain! Back to my Cranes...some are still bathing...dip and shake, then smooth the feathers with that long bill. Cries overhead and more Cranes begin the downward spiral. By mid-April they'll all be gone to their breeding grounds at Grays Lake in Idaho and points north.

Haven't seen the Bald Eagle pair for nearly two weeks, but the Northern Harriers have laid claim to the northeast pond. Another "which-is-it-duck"...all brown and gray...Gadwall I guess. Still another duck...but I recognize the "racing stripe" that continues from the white body up into the neck...and there's the long pointy tail...a Northern Pintail. Out on the main reservoir to the south, along the far shore...Western Grebes with their white bodies and black backs...and still plenty of white and black Mergansers. But there's something smaller among the tules...white body, dark head with a white splotch...Bufflehead! I count three. Trim and stylish little Ducks, less than a foot long with a wing span of nearly 2 1/2-feet...there are the brownish females. These small Ducks winter south into Mexico and nest far to our north in woodlands near water with the nest preferably in a tree  cavity. I've seen videos of the young falling out of the nest cavity into the water...tough to be a chick! Although they have a long-term pair-bond, the female seems to do most of the work. Their diet is primarily aquatic insects and such, although fish are an important food source in the winter months.

Now I see a flash of white...one of the males is displaying. Focus the scope...head thrown back, almost to touch his back...now up into normal position...then stretch forward.

My, but he's quick! He swims about vigorously...the females
don't even bother to look up. Now two more males join
him...practice time, I guess. I
appreciate their efforts
because now I'll always recognize those flashes of white that
indicate Bufflehead display.

Ah, I hear a Killdeer...there it is...and two Yellowlegs with
their grayish bodies atop long yellow legs...I think that they're
one of the best-named shorebirds. I relish these moments when
the first shorebirds appear. Later, as the reservoir's drawn down
for its designed purpose of irrigation, the shimmering water to
the south will become a natural mud-flat, great for shorebirds
as they follow the receding waterline, but often out of spotting
scope range for me. And now back to the hilltop for a final
check...over 800 Sandhill Cranes in the pasture and along the
near shoreline. Hope they have a secure night's rest.

CANADA GOOSE

There's more open water today and a good number of the local Canada Geese are swimming about here in Confluence Park lake in Delta. Of course, some are sleeping or preening or just loafing. Life seems so easy for these big birds...nearly 4-feet-long with a 6-foot wing span, outranked only by the Swan. I recall seeing them back in the 1960s when life was not so easy and these birds were rare to infrequent: at the Ruby Marsh in Nevada we watched a family climb up an embankment, cross the road, and go down the other side. At first we saw the gander's black head and bill, then the unmistakable white "chin strap," and next the long, black neck. The large body with its light breast and darker back appeared and, finally, the heavy

black legs and feet. Eight young, in single file, with the female as rearguard. Obviously such a large bird is worth the hunt, so overhunting plus loss of wetland habitat had taken its toll. Then game management, wetland recovery, and reintroduction stabilized the population. Over population has become such a problem that these birds are often considered a nuisance. The obvious question: What happened? A summary by Heather Lutz (University of Michigan) points out that these Geese are tolerant of humans and that our parks, golf courses, and such provide good habitat where the only major predators are local dogs. People feed the birds and, being social creatures, when one family finds easy city-pickings, they remember, and then return with their young, plus flock mates who in turn, remember, and the migrants become residents. There are products that make the grass less palatable to the Geese, but, in a brief Internet search, I found Barbara Ray Ligon's Goose dogs in Virginia (Seclusival Farm and Kennel). These Border collies are trained to round up and control problem Geese, so if you're a Border collie fan, check out this interesting web site.

Though the varieties of Canada Goose is obvious in any field guide, the newer *Sibley Guide to Birds* clearly pictures the major races that range from about 2-feet in length (the Aleutian, Cackling, Dusky, and Richardson's) to the Lesser at 3-feet and the Common at nearly 4-feet, with the scientific label of *Branta canadensis*: "branta" comes from the Anglo Saxon "brannan" (to burn), probably from the birds' darkish plumage. Most of these birds migrated from the north (Canada) to the south, hence the term Canada Geese, but a reasonable designation could as well be Canadian Geese. Thus far, I've found no specific reason for the "proper" label of "Canada," which is given in all recognized field guides. At two or three years of age, they form long-term pair-bonds and often return to the area of their birth. They can fly at 70 m.p.h. and attain an altitude of 9,000 feet. Formidable birds, indeed.

To quote Aldo Leopold in Wisconsin, "One swallow does not a summer make, but one skein of geese, cleaving the murk of a March thaw, is the spring." And as I gaze at these majestic, but half-domesticated Geese, a wonderful childhood memory comes to me: being wakened from my warm bed, quickly bundled up, and hurried into the cold night air. And overhead, against a clear, bright, moonlit sky, was a wedge of honking Canada Geese heading north in a Colorado March.

April Fool's, 1997

I can barely make out the gray of Sandhill Cranes in the field...yesterday morning I estimated over 2,000 birds. I watched on and off all day long as they tried to leave, only to be battered by the wind and snow. Last evening I estimated about 1,300 here at Hart's Basin, so a few hundred did not return. I can't help but wonder how far they went, for this is a major storm, covering our entire region...I hope that they found a safe roost for the night.

The storm arrived on March 31, continued through yesterday and today. The visibility is very poor...I can hardly see Vela's ranch house only half a mile below. The trees down at the dam are lost in the flying snow. Some April Fool's! Thus far we've had over 10,000 Cranes stay overnight with us this season, and there's not much left to eat now. A squall hits...back into the car

to get warm! And I clearly recall thinking, when we first came to this area, that I'd just drive up to Crane Point and have a look...a friend said, "Oh, that's an innocent enough pursuit." And here I am, wondering what I'm doing out here in this blizzard. But of course, I know...I'm enamored with Cranes and now with all the other birds that migrate through here or who choose to nest at Hart's Basin each summer.

What I'd seen of Crane behavior during these migrations had been interesting...I'd learned to spot the mated pairs and a family (a mated pair plus last season's young). I'd watched them bathing and preening and roosting in the shallow water. But yesterday's observations were fascinating and dreadful at the same time. No Cranes were loafing: Instead, they were all searching for food. None were just walking around: They were annoyed with anything that came into their little personal space. Calm Cranes became aggressive Cranes, charging at the supposed intruder with lowered head and outspread wings. Even in the poor light I could see the inflated red crowns, a sure sign of distress. A few had lowered themselves to the ground...to rest or simply to endure? The snow and the wind never stopped. And to compound their troubles, a Golden Eagle, the arch predator of Cranes, had been perched on the hilltop since the storm began.

Surely they can't get airborne in this soup...but a few are in the pre-flight stance...and there they go. Out of the car with the binoculars...the birds are buffeted, blown sideways, pushed backwards...head-on they go into the blizzard. Most return...brutal. I'll never hear that old saying "free as a bird" but this scene will spring into my mind.

Though there is little to no food, these tough birds will survive and continue to the nesting grounds. But the storm will take its toll. Some will be weakened and die, others will not have sufficient reserves to nest and raise their chick. As I scurry back into the warmth of the car, the drama in Vela's field continues. But I'm near-froze and it's past time to be home.

Post script: On the morning of April 4, 1997, approximately 1,000 Cranes took off into clearing weather. The storm had entrapped them for four days.

Early Summer

Bindweed
Convolvulus arvensis

EARED GREBE

The wind has died down...mirror-calm now all across Hart's Basin. From the pull-out along the northwest ponds, I can see five large, gray shapes...Great Blue Heron standing atop their nests in the heronry by the dam...it's that time of year.

On down to the eastern end...with the spotting scope I can make out a group of Shovelers out toward the middle...swimming in circles to stir up food. Coots are abundant...several swimming along with that chicken-like head-bobbing. As a rule of thumb, when the Cranes have passed through, the Grebes arrive. So now...the shrill call of the black and white Western Grebes echoes across the water...elegant birds with trim bodies and long necks...small swans in tuxedoes. They nest in the east shore tules. The grunt-like call of the little Pied-billed Grebe...short body, short neck, mottled gray bill...not at all Grebe-like...Hart's Basin nesters, too.

A soft splash...about twenty feet from the road...the ripples widen. Didn't sound like a fish...wait and watch...nothing. The trees on the far side are filled with Yellow-headed Blackbirds. Movement on the water behind me...just a glimpse of a bird's rump...diving. Watch again...nothing. Could it be an Eared Grebe? They can stay submerged for up to three minutes and travel as far as fifty feet underwater...move the scope out of the way to get a broader view with my binoculars. There it is...gone before I can focus...it was about a foot-long,

darkish color, with a splash of bright feathers on the head. It emerges about twenty feet down to my right...the neck is black but the eye is red...a characteristic of the Grebes.

Now it drifts along, the belly seems reddish...the feathers sweeping back from the red eye are golden, fine as hairs...very pretty! Down again...then up, on the other side of the roadside shrub. I'd have to move the car or get out and that would be disturbing to my bird...let him feed.

These birds inhabit parts of Eurasia, Africa, and North America. Ours winter along the West Coast and into Mexico. They nest in the United States and Canada with the highest breeding populations occurring in the pothole marshes of Manitoba. In her *Guide to Colorado Birds,* Mary Taylor Gray lists North Park, the San Luis Valley, and our eastern plains as nesting sites. From the descriptions given, the Eared Grebe's complex courtship displays are similar to that of our Hart's Basin Western Grebes.

While the male watches, the female builds the nest, often in the shelter of cattails and tules. Both adults incubate the eggs in a shallow, floating nest. The eggs may actually rest below water level and when the adults leave, they cover the eggs with wet vegetation. Soggy way to start life! But the chicks are downy, mobile, follow the adults and hitch rides upon their parents' backs. All Grebes are fish eaters and all dive in pursuit of fish. The fins and bones are difficult to digest, which leads to a curious feeding practice: The adults eat feathers and feed feathers to their young. The hypothesis: Feathers cushion the innards from the sharp bones. Research has shown that up to fifty percent of the stomach contents may be feather balls. And the question arises: Why didn't they evolve a better digestive system? Something to keep researchers busy and bird-watchers curious.

My bird is here again...near the road...seems distressed but doesn't fly. Instead it sinks slowly below the surface, a typical Grebe maneuver. How did it do that? Interesting behavior and a beautiful bird. They're infrequent spring migrants here, and I always feel privileged to see the handsome little Eared Grebe.

Tule
Scinus acutus

AMERICAN AVOCET

I can see birds moving behind the near-shore willows...one...now two. About 1 1/2 feet-long...body's smaller than that of a Canada Goose. Now two more appear...they're all legs and neck. They're  foraging along the water's edge...dipping their long bills into the water...now an unusual sideways swinging of the head back and forth...as if they are sweeping the water. Obviously getting something to eat. Back in the BB days (Before Birding), I'd seen pictures of such birds but couldn't identify them in their natural setting. Now I immediately know that they're American Avocet. What a sense of accomplishment!

Down to the causeway for a closer look...beautiful! Pure white bodies with broad black areas on the sides...the heads and necks have a russet orange wash. It's often difficult to be sure of leg color in shorebirds because they tend to be disguised by mud! But on this sunny day the legs are obviously blue-gray. The length of the black, needle thin bills is at least three times the width of the heads. I've read that they feed by feel as they sweep the bill along or just beneath the water's surface...but one of these seems to be chasing insects on the surface. And

suddenly they're in flight...as they pass above me the bodies are white while the wingtips are black...don't seem disturbed by my presence...I can't see a reason for their flight. Over the roadway, across the northwest pond and then turning...the black-white pattern on their upper bodies is striking. Now they return to this shoreline...landing gracefully. They continue feeding as if nothing had disturbed them.

Although these common shorebirds can be found across much of our continent, their beauty always impresses me. The range map indicates nesting grounds into Canada with wintering grounds into Mexico. At Hart's Basin, Avocet are common in small numbers during the warm months but they nest in the Great Basin region to our west. The *Birder's Handbook* describes courtship as bowing, crouching, and dancing with wings spread. Both parents build the nest that is a mere scrape among tufts of shoreline vegetation or on gravel, sand, or a mud-flat. It's lined with bits of grass or mud chips and houses three or four 1-inch eggs. For the first few days, the female incubates the eggs and then the male finishes the job. The young are downy, mobile, and follow the parents to find their own food. And they'll fly in about thirty days. It would be worth a trip to the Salt Lake area to see them at nest.

Avocet is a pretty word as intriguing as the bird itself. Italian "avocetta" refers to long-legged shorebirds with upturned bills which led to the scientific name of *Recurvirostra*

(Latin for "bent" and "rostrum" for "bill"). So, since it's a European word, it follows that there must be Avocets in Europe and, sure enough, they're included in my new book, *Birds of Britain and Europe*. They're similar to ours, but there's no orange coloring and the top of the head is black. I recall exploring the Internet on a stormy winter's day and discovering that there are four species of Avocet: one occurring throughout Europe, Asia, and Africa; another in South America; one in Australia; and our North American bird, *Recurvirostra americana*. The scientific description mentioned that the front toes are webbed...can't see that feature on these birds...been watching for a couple of years without any luck. Last fall I observed similar looking birds that lacked the orange wash and finally realized that they were American Avocet in winter plumage...just as elegant as these birds are today.

BLACK-NECKED STILT

The sky's clear and light breezes ruffle the water. The only ducks left are likely to be nesters: Mallards, Pintails, Redheads, and Green-winged Teal. It's a good time to watch for shorebirds, but by habit I always watch for Sandhill Cranes...saw two a few days ago and hope that they stay around like the pair did a couple of years ago. But no Cranes today.

Pull off the road on the west end of the reservoir and there's no need for my spotting scope...Black-necked Stilt! What a treat! They occur here each year, but the sightings are few and far between. I've played a bit with the Internet this winter and, thanks to www.saltgrassflats.com, I discovered that this bird weighs all of 6-ounces. My bird's just at the edge of the grass...the back is a shiny black that goes up the back of its neck into a black-topped head...the white splotch above the black eye is very obvious. The under-side is pure white...the black bill needle-thin...a black and white bird trimmed with pencil-thin red legs. A Stilt when disturbed is a noisy bird, hence the common name of "Lawyer Bird." Now it's quiet...there it goes, chasing after bugs on the surface of the water. Amazing how quickly it can run with such long legs.

I've read that only the Flamingo exceeds it in leg to body ratio.

In general size and style, it's a lot like the Avocet, which turns out to be closely related. In fact, Fred Ryser, in his *Birds of the Great Basin*, says that the two nest together in loose colonies. The Stilt's nest is a mere scrape lined with sticks, plant parts, and mud chips along alkaline, marshy areas. Both parents help build the nest, incubate (about twenty-five days), and care for the chicks until they can fly (another twenty or so days). The chicks are mobile, downy, follow the adults, and can find their own food (precocious or, in birder-talk, "precocial"). Though the web site shows juveniles, the best presentation I've found is in the new *Sibley Guide to Birds*: The young birds look like the adult, except that the black of the back does not go up the neck. The breeding range goes along the Atlantic coast into South America, and includes the western United States, with a few pair in the San Luis Valley and at the Arapaho NWR near Walden.

Fred Ryser's book on Great Basin birds is one of the most fascinating volumes that I've ever found. He describes the adult Stilt "kneeling," holding its body parallel to the ground in order to provide shade for the chicks, and in hot weather the adult transports water in its feathers to cool the eggs or chicks by a "belly-soaking." It may make a hundred trips a day. It would be wonderful to visit one of the nesting sites some spring.

But my bird takes flight, black-white against the blue sky with red legs trailing behind. It seems to be headed for the far end of the reservoir. I'd follow but it's getting late...never enough time. But I've had a very good look at my Black-necked Stilt here at Hart's Basin.

WILSON'S PHALAROPE

It's nice to have some sunshine after the days of monsoon rains. The moisture, always welcome, will help our little reservoir fill. But the shoreline, where the water meets the mud-flat, is a long way off. I can make out movement but can only be sure of the larger birds, such as the Great Blue Herons and the Canada Geese.

Through the spotting scope I can see that the mud-flats at the upper end are still dry. Canada Geese...about seventy, plus the two white-escaped domestics. At least twenty Great Blue Herons on both shores and along the inlet. I wonder how many will fledge from this year's nests in the cottonwoods near the dam. Ducks and Coots in the wet-weed patches...elegant Western Grebes in the open water.

There's movement far off, on the eastern end of the reservoir. Looks small...white...Avocet? Yes, four of them, elegant as ever. Now I see a disturbance on the far south shore...a flock of birds lifts into the air...wheel as a single unit...white bellies flashing in the sun. They turn, showing their dark backs and vanishing against the background of sagebrush and greasewood. I never tire of this shorebird show of "now you see it, now you don't."

The flock turns toward the near shore...Killdeer? No. They land and the behavior is busy, busy, busy...so they're Phalaropes. Now turn up the magnification...they scurry about in the mud...the long narrow bills about equal to the head width...they're clearly gray and white rather than the brown-white of Killdeer. And the necks are much too long. They're Phalaropes for sure.

These 8-inch shorebirds breed in our northern states or into Canada and we have nesters here at Hart's Basin, though I've never been lucky enough to see the chicks. They winter in the shallow, alkaline ponds of western South America.

Among birders, the Phalaropes are noted for their unusual reversal of sex roles. The female courts the male and then chooses one of the nest sites that he has prepared, usually on moist ground that is often surrounded by water. After the first egg is laid, he lines the scrape with grasses and such. She continues laying until there are three or four eggs, and then she deserts him. The male incubates the eggs and tends the young. Both sexes have a black "racing stripe" which extends from the bill back through the eye and down the neck. It fades to red and then extends along the back. The female's markings are much more colorful than the male's, and she is a bit larger as well. Both sexes fade to gray above and white beneath in non-breeding plumage.

Our Wilson's Phalarope is named in honor of the nine-teenth-century ornithologist, Thomas Wilson. The three colors found in the breeding plumage of the female (white body with reddish tones trimmed in black) give the scientific label of *Phalaropus tricolor.* There are two Phalaropes in Europe. The Gray Phalarope is all gray in winter plumage but all red in breeding plumage (it's sometimes given the common name of Red

Phalarope in American field guides). There's also the Red-necked, which occurs on our continent, but only as a migrant. And I was thrilled to see it at Hart's Basin in the spring of 2001. But our Wilson's Phalarope seems to be unique to our continent and does not occur in Eurasia.

I find names to be fascinating, and the Phalarope's name led me to our common Coot. Huh? My dictionary of bird names gave two Greek words: "phalaris" (Coot) plus "pous" (foot), to create the name of phalaropus. And, strangely enough, this led me to life-styles: Some birds, such as ducks, that are primarily 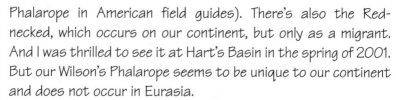 swimmers have webbing between their toes (think paddles). Other birds, such as Robins, that live on land and perch in trees have separate toes. But there is an in-between life-style, such as that of the Coot: It swims a good deal but also scrambles about on the shore and attempts to perch in shoreline shrubs. So the Coot has "in-between" feet: The toes are still separate but each segment is lobed, thus providing swim-ability and perch-ability. And the guides gave the Red-necked Phalarope as *Phalaropus lobatus*. For it's lobed feet? But the trail ended there: I need another reference! I've seen the odd feet of Coots, and now I'll watch for a Phalarope's feet when they're walking about on the shore. Another dimension in the fascinating study of birds.

Phalaropes are famous for their unique feeding method: They spin around rapidly to churn up the water and then eat the resultant aquatic insects and vegetation. But there's no time to watch for "spinning top" behavior today. Lightning flashes over Grand Mesa...thunder...the storm's headed my way. Time to leave.

KILLDEER

Our group begins to gather in front of Bill Heddles Recreation Center for a leisurely walk in Delta's Confluence Park to celebrate National Trails Day. I hear the lonesome "peep-peep" of Killdeer...there, at the edge of the lawn just past the flag poles. I pause to chat with some folks and then can't relocate the bird at all. Now, walking toward the Gunnison River, we see more Killdeer in the lawn areas. Most are busy foraging for insects and their presence is always welcome, since insects make up about seventy-five percent of their diet.

This common bird is about the size of a Robin but has long, light-colored legs. Probably our best known shorebird, it's brown above and white beneath, with two black neck bands, a black cap, a black-brown line under the eye. There's a white line from the eye to the back of the head. These black lines break up the bird's silhouette as it stands or moves in the open, arid terrain that it prefers. Other birds of this group, the Plovers, also have similar bands but, interestingly, our Killdeer is the largest and it has two bands while the other Plovers have only one band. And the juvenile Killdeer, smaller of course, has only one band but grows a second band as it matures. I recall seeing a one-band-plover at Hart's

Basin, which I took to be the Semipalmated Plover that may migrate through our area. But it turned out to be a young Killdeer, not really a disappointment at all!

Approaching the Gunnison River, we stop at the large, glass-covered interpretive sign that shows the Great Blue Heron. Sadly the new nesting tree across the river is not nearly as obvious as the old one was. But a Heron and its nest are clearly visible to those who brought their binoculars. Hear Mourning Dove and the raucous squawk of Yellow-headed Blackbird as we turn toward the wetland area. Here at the edge of the wetland we hear the distant Delta traffic, feel the breeze and the warmth of the sun. Hear a woodpecker drumming...and I hear a warbler-like song, too.

But we turn to walk through the wooded area and then back onto the lake shore where we spot another Killdeer loafing at the water's edge. They're resident through much of the United States and this one looks so innocent, almost lazy. But it may have spent some summers far into northern Canada and seen winters in central South America. Long migrations, indeed.

These birds tolerate humans and many of us have seen their famous distraction display of a broken wing. The purpose of the display is to lure predators away from its nest, which is a mere scrape in the ground. In *Birds of the Great Basin*, Fred Ryser discusses displays: The nearer to hatching time or if young are at the nest site, the more vigorous the displays, since this time is the culmination of the pair's investment in the nest. If the broken wing display doesn't work, the bird may run about until it finds a depression in the ground and there squat down as if on a nest...such behavior is termed "dummy nest." Most amazing, the bird may sit on the real nest until the adversary is very close and then fly up in its face. But apparently this bird is not yet guarding a nest, so no display for us today.

The scrape that serves as a nest is often lined or camouflaged with gravel, pebbles, and such. The literature mentions that part of the courtship is pebble-tossing. Something new to watch for. Here's another Killdeer in the path ahead...run...stop and peep...run. It's time to end our walk, but it has been a delightful morning in celebration of Trails Day.

RED-WINGED BLACKBIRDS

The sky's overcast, but there's little wind. A few Mallards and Canada Geese along the small ditch this side of the Bureau of Reclamation's fence. Along the near shore, the water's nearly covered with Mallards...some Northern Pintails. Lots of birds further out in the main reservoir...a few Common Mergansers, the males with their shining white bodies and dark heads and the females with gray-bodies, white-breasts, and reddish heads. But they are out-numbered by the elegant black-white Western Grebes, who are beginning to set up their nest sites for the season here at the Basin.

Here are the colorful Green-winged Teal in the northeast pond. They've often been mistaken for the Wood Duck, which usually doesn't occur here. And Red-winged Blackbirds are singing in the cattails, staking out their territories. Nearer the road, the dark-brown females with their streaked breasts sit quietly in the tules. When these birds appear at our feeders in winter, the females always trick me...I think, what a big sparrow! Then it turns out to be a female Redwing. The adjacent cattails are

thick with male Redwings. I've read that the males gather in groups away from the juveniles and females in fall, winter, and early spring, but there are females mixed in these flocks...so the season's hurrying right along. This winter I read that Yellow-headed Blackbirds occupy the safer, deep-water portions of a marsh while the Redwings occupy the shallower areas...something to watch for this season. Another flock flies into the trees right by the road.

Two males scrambling in the tamarisk at the edge of the road...flashes of red...then one settles on a lower branch and the other perches near the top...neither shows red, only a yellowish streak along the shoulder is visible...dispute settled? I've known Red-winged Blackbirds most of my life, but never realized that the male's red wing patch could be covered or flashed at will as a dominance or territorial display. No matter how long I've known a bird, there's always something new to learn about it at Hart's Basin.

High Summer

Fireweed
Epilobium augustifolium

GREAT EGRET

From Crane Point, I can see the storm clouds boil about the Uncompahgre Plateau. Canyons appear, then vanish. Buttes and mesas seem to move within the storm. Lightning and thunder over Cedar Mesa...looks like I won't have much time. A pipeline, held down with rocks, crosses the reservoir and then goes up to the top of Antelope Hill. It serves as my measuring device as the water's drawn down for irrigation each season. Except where it's silted over, the pipeline is completely exposed now and the main body of water is considerably below it. The birds are a long way off and I have to use the spotting scope all the time.

About ten Great Blue Herons along the near shore...on the far side are another ten. Along the inlet from the causeway or North Road and down to the water itself, I can make out another twenty Blues...so about forty for today. Wait...there's a white bird among them, same size and shape as the Great Blue Herons...Great Egret? Magnification up and I can imagine that I see dark legs and pale-colored bill...the neck is held in an "S" curve...like the Great Blues but, they often pull their necks down into hunched shoulders. This is a Great Egret...it walks into the water, then begins to stalk fish, just like the Great Blues. Both of these species will eat just about anything: insects, crawfish, reptiles, amphibians, small mammals, and young birds. But here they eat lots of our extremely plentiful carp.

We've had a Great Egret at Hart's Basin for most of this summer. In her *Guide to Colorado Birds*, Gray includes the Snowy Egret and the Cattle Egret (both seen at Hart's Basin), but she does not include our Great Egret at all. The unpublished Bird List for the Basin includes our bird as rare in spring and fall but present in summer (possibly breeding). In my few years of observation, I've never seen any indication of breeding pairs: What a treat that would be! In his "Courtship and Pair Formation in the Great Egret," Jochen Wiese discusses the birds' behaviors in the southeastern United States. The male arrives to establish territory, builds or repairs a platform of sticks and twigs from which he displays to the arriving females. He accepts one, they continue the courtship, and three or so 2-inch eggs are laid. Both birds incubate and tend the chicks, who are born immobile but downy with eyes open. At about three weeks they leave the nest to forage in juvenile groups until they can fly, in about forty days. I've read that such colonies may number in the thousands of birds.

All Egrets develop extravagant plumage during the breeding season, and the beautiful feathers led to the birds' near extinction during the late 1800s. It was fashionable to wear fancy feathers, especially on ladies' hats. An ounce of Egret feathers sold for $32 (about four-birds worth): twice the price of an ounce of gold. Later the price rocketed to $80 an ounce. Birds were hunted and killed and, of course, this was most easily accomplished while they were on the nest, hence their young died as well. This slaughter of Egrets and a host of other birds brought about a counter movement for conservation, and among these groups were the American Ornithologists Union and the Audubon Society with their emblem of the Egret.

Many of my books list the Great Egret as *Casmerodius albus*. The first part of the name means brother or sister to "erodios," which is Greek for "heron." So, the Great Egret is akin to the herons. That's true. And the Latin term "albus" means white. But this label mixes Greek and Latin. The new name, *Ardea alba,* uses the only Latin terms: "ardea" meaning "heron" and "alba" for "white." At first I was annoyed at the name change, but now that I understand the reasoning behind the new name, I am more comfortable with "*Ardea alba.*" Even ornithologists like to be tidy.

As I gaze at this beautiful bird, I realize that, as the most cosmopolitan of the Egrets, its kind may be found throughout the world except for the Far North. My particular bird may spend the winter on our coastlines or as far south as Central America. I'm amazed at the bird's strength and endurance as well as at its stately beauty.

Swallows

There are plenty of birds today...at least twenty Great Blue Herons...Canada Geese in the grassy areas...several elegant Western Grebes in the deeper water. The bright green wet-weed patches are alive with ducks...and the black Coots with their white faces.

Drive down to the causeway for a closer look. The upper parts of the reservoir are still wet...must be from all the recent rain. With the scope I can make out distant birds...black-white Avocet with the orangish wash down their necks. And near at hand there are small birds perched along the fence line...a few

take flight...then more and in moments a host of Swallows fills the sky above me! They flit and turn...pivot and glide...taking insects on the wing. I've read that they spend more time airborne than any other songbird and are rarely seen on the ground, though some species do consume berries and seeds. Occasionally I get a glimpse of metallic blue-green. The birds are too swift for me to track with the scope...try with the binoculars...too far away to tell much but their numbers are impressive. At least a hundred birds. Some move eastward and they land together in the dark green of the tules.

Try again with the scope while they are sitting...some have white breasts...others with reddish breasts...and there's the tan-gray breast of the Rough-winged Swallow. Off they go again...there's the distinctive reddish breast and forked tail of the Barn Swallow. I recall that it's the only one with a "swallow tail:" The tails of the other five species of our region are merely notched. Plain blue-green metallic back, Tree Swallow...a glimpse of white patches into the metallic green of the lower back, Violet-green Swallow for sure.

Four species identified at this distance...not bad. Swallows are not easy to distinguish since all members of this worldwide family of insect eaters are about the same size (5 or 6-inches long), have small legs, long pointed wings, small bills, and large mouths. Ours, summering throughout the United States and Canada, will soon be gathering for their fall migrations to Central and South America. I've been told that the related Purple Martins are in our area, and I've also been told that there aren't any. But I've never encountered one that I knew for sure to be a Purple Martin. So, I'll have to add them to the long list of "birds that aren't here, but maybe they are."

I recall bits of information as I watch these acrobatic flyers.

Those less likely to be seen at Hart's Basin are the Bank Swallow and the Cliff Swallow. Most Swallows tend to be monogamous, that is, they stay together for at least one season...they often nest in fairly large colonies except for Rough-winged. The Cliff and Barn build mud-based nests, which can often be seen along cliff faces, under bridges, along barn eaves, or in various other structures. The Violet-green and Tree Swallows are cavity dwellers and sometimes utilize birdhouses. The Bank and Rough-winged prefer burrows within, you guessed it, a stream bank.

Ouch! I knew that mosquitoes were here before I stopped the car...Swallow activity usually indicates the need for insect repellent. Since insects are the primary diet of these swift-flying birds, they are always welcome. And I know that each species is a story in itself, but I've no time to read the field guide! The elegant flyers dip and dive over the reservoir, demanding my attention. Select one bird...a Violet-green, because I can better track the white patches that reach into his back...try to follow with my binoculars. Down to the water's surface...up and away to the east...now south...down to the water again...now north...back toward me. It's much easier to study them when they're sitting on a wire!

Suddenly the sun vanishes behind a growing cloud bank to the west. This evening of clear sky above, mirror-calm water below, and clouds of Swallows has been a treasure.

MALLARD

A duck is a duck is a duck. Or, if it looks like a duck and sounds like a duck, it probably is a duck. Oh, if life were only that simple! But every species has its own unique set of vocalizations. We tend to think of ducks as saying "quack," but the only one that goes "quack" is the female Mallard, and her mate has a reedy, soft voice. And since these Ducks are very common, appearing anywhere and whenever there's a bit of open water, they (or rather she) is the one that we hear, and so we tune out the other duck calls. This species occurs in marshes and wetlands, and on ponds, lakes, and reservoirs, including those bodies of water on our Grand Mesa.

They belong to a large group called "dabbling ducks," for they dabble or dip into shallow water for aquatic vegetation and insects. Other members of their tribe include the Teals, Pintails, Shovelers, and Wigeons. We  often see these ducks with rumps pointing toward the sky: a perfect time to note the male Mallard's curly tail. This single, distinctive characteristic occurs in our barnyard ducks because they are descended from the Mallards that were domesticated long ago in China and in the Near East. In his *Birds of the Great Basin*, Fred Ryser points out that today our domesticated ducks hybridize with their living wild ancestors and so create the plentitude of strange-looking ducks in our parks.

In the wild, courtship begins in fall and winter to create a single season pair-bond before spring's nesting time. Ryser includes a detailed description of these ritualized behaviors. For example, the female incites her mate against another male. The males string together a number of behaviors such as head shaking, turning, nodding, head pumping, and vigorous bathing. The next time you observe these very common Mallards, perhaps you'll want to pause a bit to see what they're doing. You may recognize these behaviors.

The hen selects the nest site, often in a grassy area near water. When egg laying begins, she pulls down from her breast to line the nest and covers the eggs during her forays to feed, drink, and bathe. When incubation begins (requiring about a month), the male leaves her to join bachelor flocks of molting, flightless males. If one must become flightless, this is a convenient time, since she cannot leave the chicks. And so the female also molts as she tends her young. The chicks are downy, mobile, and able to find food by themselves. Although the primary diet is stems and seeds of aquatic plants, Mallards have acquired a taste for agricultural crops. Because they are often in large flocks, they may even be responsible for crop depredation.

In many areas, including Delta, Mallards can be found all year, so we can rightly call them "resident." They nest at Hart's Basin and on up to the ponds and lakes of Grand Mesa. I'm accustomed to seeing these familiar Ducks among the cattails and tules of the Basin, and it always gives me a bit of a start to see them along the edges of high-elevation ponds edged with Fireweed and Gooseberries. Others nest far into Canada or

Alaska and winter into central Mexico. Much scientific study has been done on these common Ducks. But while most of us note the date of the first Pintail or Wigeon, we often fail to even notice the Mallards. Perhaps you'll take time to observe them in our area. So, "happy ducking."

AMERICAN PIPIT

GOVERNOR'S BASIN

We're still well above timberline. My friend, Marian, points out that the jeep trail behind us rises to cross over the top of Black Bear Pass and weave its tortuous way down to Telluride to the west. And our guides remind me that our jeep trail (down the east side of the pass) is much less difficult than Black Bear. But it's more than exciting enough for me!

We still have a little time before starting back to Ouray, and I'm checking Janet Wingate's *Alpine Flower Finder* to be certain that I've noted my new alpine "finds" for the day: the ones that are no longer just pictures in the book but are now in my memory-file forever. Here's the little gray inconspicuous Boreal Sage, and all across the slope below us is a spectacular display Old-Man-of-The-Mountain with its bright yellow, 3-inch-wide flower atop its 5-inch stem. Today I've found the Pink-headed Daisy, the Silky Phacelia, Macauleyi's Buttercup with its dense coat of dark brown hairs, Alpine Avens with its lovely yellow rose-like flowers, and the snapdragon-like white blossoms of James' Snowlover. And the long-sought Alp Lily. There are several more new flowers, each one precious, but the clouds threaten and it's time to go down off the mountain. The tundra's "belly-flowers" are reminiscent of the desert flora that led me into botany: Both regions are arid (here the moisture is frozen and inaccessible to plants for most of the year), but the controlling factor is the cold rather than the desert's heat.

Our route is fairly level for a while, passing through an undulating area of snow banks, dry soils, and cushion plants. Many of the rocks are barren, sharp, and angular, but others are covered with lichens in an amazing variety of colors: deep reds, yellows, brilliant orange, grays, greens, and pale blues. In the damp nooks and crannies are miniature forests of mosses.

There's movement on a patch of snow to our right. Chip, our expert driver, stops for us...it's a small bird. Sparrow? About  that size but a slimmer silhouette...tail is longer...bill's slender and pointed like an insect-eater. Someone calls out "Water Pipit." I don't know that bird well, but the name seems right. The bird is walking rather than hopping. The gait is more like a stride...chasing something...snatches up a wiggling form and takes flight. I glimpse a white-margined tail...our bird vanishes downslope.

As we continue downward I try to recall the bird...no eyering or wing bars, dark legs, and large feet. The breast and eyeline were pale with a pinkish hue. Rather than eating the insect our bird flew away with it, probably to feed its young. It's hard to concentrate amidst such gorgeous mountain wildflowers and stunning waterfalls. Occasionally we get glimpses of Highway 550: The summit of Red Mountain Pass is far below us.

Later, in the comfort of Marian Fick's lovely home, I check my old copy of *The Golden Guide to Birds of North America* and confirm the bird as a Water Pipit. The range maps show summer or nesting through Alaska, Canada's Northwest Territories, and southward into the Rocky Mountains. My *Birder's Handbook* tells me that the female bird builds a shallow grass/twig nest on open tundra with both parents tending the young. The birds prefer to forage in moist areas or shallow water: The name comes from their association with water and their piping call. They consume crustaceans, insects, seeds, and berries...a melting snow bank would certainly be suitable. And, this bird was walking rather than hopping, another bit of confirmation that correlates with the book.

There are several species of Pipit in Europe and Asia where they're found in wintering flocks along beaches, pastures, and fields. Our Pipit winters as far south in winter as Guatemala and El Salvador. I first met this small bird at a refuge in Nevada and it was listed as *Anthus spinoletta*: a pretty name for a pretty little bird. There are several such little birds in the genus "anthus," but the name merely refers to small birds that were mentioned by Pliny (first-century Roman naturalist). Similarly, "spinoletta" is

Alp Lily
Lloydia serotina

Italian for some little bird (unknown to us!). But our Pipit now has a new name. It's now American Pipit instead of Water Pipit and has the scientific label of *Anthus rubescens*: To me, that term doesn't really fit because it means "reddish," and my bird was merely pinkish. Oh, well. This time the new scientific name doesn't help me any more than the old name did.

During courtship, the male floats down above the female, singing all the way. It's easy to imagine this delightful display.

The ground nest is constructed with an overhang of rock or vegetation and takes four or five days to build. In this cold climate, there's clearly only time for one brood. As the pointed bill suggests, these 6-inch birds consume insects, as well as some seeds, crustaceans, and berries. They are described with the northern nesting Wagtails (named for their tail wagging!). The book indicates that today's Pipit could likely wag its tail, too. But I didn't get to see that.

Though I'd first seen this little bird along a lakeshore and then once in an urban park, now my recollection of American or Water Pipit will be along this snow bank in Governor's Basin.

AMERICAN WHITE PELICAN

As I turn right at the intersection of Highway 65 and North Road, I leave the beautiful Presbyterian Church and the Big E Store behind. Traveling east for about a mile brings me to Hart's Basin. And it looks like August...the ponds to the north of the causeway are filled in with vegetation instead of water. To the south, a broad mud-flat extends into the reservoir and the large wet-weed patch is high and dry. As the reservoir recedes with our irrigation needs, it becomes unsightly to human eyes, but the birds don't mind at all. With my binoculars I can see geese, ducks, shorebirds, and Western Grebes. Most surprising are large white birds...very large white birds.

Down to the causeway for a better look...and yes, indeed, our American White Pelicans are still with us! It's always a pleasure to see them here, but since these huge birds migrate and nest across our continent, it's not really  unusual. These Pelicans began to appear in April and, by the end of the month, a small flock of eight were commonly seen. Since then there has regularly been a flock varying from a few birds to over fifty. Four years ago we had a big flock of these Pelicans throughout the summer, but in other years only a few appeared. The young join together in groups called "pods" and, since their arrival in May here at Hart's Basin, most of these birds have appeared to be young ones with grayish plumage and pinkish bills, rather than the clear white plumage and yellow bills of adults. I've seen only two that had the "lump on the bill," the Pelican's version of breeding plumage, but they're not here today. Though I've tried to watch carefully, I've not seen anything that looked like nesting behavior.

Park off the road and enjoy the show...five Pelicans are swimming along together...in a line. The heads are lowered so that the bills appear to be resting on the breast...neck-less Pelicans. Now the lead bird tenses...head stretching forward and bill stabbing downward. Then head up and gulp! It's tough to be a fish. The second bird dips its head beneath the surface...the head turns to the side...the bird swings around but apparently "no catch." The last bird raises its head from the water...I can glimpse movement inside the pouch...head back and the catch is swallowed.

Most of the other Pelicans are resting along the inlet shore...I count twenty-five. Some are sleeping...others just sitting and a few are standing. One stretches the wings...a big bird, over 4-feet-long. It reaches back, smoothing the tail feathers...one wing up and it straightens the plumage underneath...extracts a single feather with that huge bill and drops it in the mud. No, the feather is stuck to the bill...now the bird walks a couple of steps and dips the bill into the water...feather's adrift. That's new behavior! Now another bird arrives, over 9-foot wing span. It glides into the flock...lands...shakes the tail and settles into place. Hope that our Pelicans stay for a while longer at Hart's Basin.

SORA

The car comes to a stop. We're off the roadway and so near the edge that I couldn't get out if I wanted to. As usual, my mouth tends to stay in gear but shifts into neutral with Dave's words, "To see a Sora, you must be as quiet as possible." I stare into the watery roots of a dying tamarisk. Nothing there. My eye drifts out to the Phalaropes foraging in the northeast pond. Still no action nearby. I must remind myself that few folks are fortunate enough to see a Sora, and that I've never seen one. Yellow-headed Blackbirds up ahead. Swallows overhead. Keep one eye on the water around the tamarisk because that's where David saw the Sora.

And all of a sudden I'm looking at a chicken-like bird with a bright-yellow, chicken-like beak. It's basically gray but the darker back feathers appear to be scalloped with white edges arranged in horizontal lines...and the scalloping goes vertically along the back half of the body...look at those legs! Bright yellow like the beak. It's dark around the face and chin...erect little tail that's black on the top side and white on the bottom. It forages around the tamarisk roots...now out of sight on the far side. Seconds pass...minutes...hours? No bird. I realize that I've forgotten to breathe! Here it comes...out onto a tussock of grass. The toes are very long and I remember that these marsh birds are built to walk on lily pads and such. Now down off the tussock...water's a bit deep and the Sora swims to the next tussock. A bit ahead of us now...around another tamarisk. Seconds...minutes...hours? But the Sora has vanished. No matter...this memory is mine forever.

Cattail
Typha latifolia

Since that marvelous moment, I've been fortunate enough to see my Sora on two more occasions. And, of course, I've found it in my books at home. This shy bird, a bit smaller than a Killdeer (6 or 7-inches-long), ranges across the North American continent and may winter through South America. It's a member of the diverse order of birds that includes Coots (seems reasonable) and the Cranes, who are also wading birds. The Rails are described as "thin" birds because they can move through the narrow spaces between the dense plant stems in their habitat, hence the saying "thin as a rail." The Sora's call is unmistakable: It seems to say "sor a...sor a" with a higher second note followed by a horse-like whinny. Having listened to it on the audio tapes that accompany the Peterson guides, I wonder that I'd never heard it here, for the Sora is listed as a breeding species on the old Hart's Basin bird list. In *Birds of the Great Basin*, Ryser mentions that the bird calls at night as well as during the day. So, another dimension to explore.

The information concerning nesting habits is fascinating. The birds remain together for the season, building their saucer-like nest a few inches above the water, and concealing it with arching vegetation. Ryser states that both parents begin incubating before all of the inch-long eggs have been laid so that the chicks hatch at different times. The female lays ten or so eggs: more than can be covered by the bird's small body. So the eggs may be placed in layers and then rotated by the adults. The chicks, little black fuzz balls with whitish legs, swim almost immediately and follow the parents. When the young are capable of independent living, the adults move away into a new area: a reversal of the usual pattern with the young leaving the nesting territory. It seems that there will always be a new bird for me at Hart's Basin.

Western Grebe

It's a pretty scene from Crane Point. The fields and pastures right below me are fresh, growing green with the big hay-rolls spaced along the fence line. Not a leaf moving on the shoreline willows or the pasture cottonwood. The fields are green but the hills beyond are all tans and grays...the distant West Elk Mountains are a study of purples. Brown-velvet seed spikes arise from the olive- green cattail beds. Against the far east shore, the tules form a 6-feet-tall band of greenish-gray with a dull bluish cast. Their tops droop with heavy tan seed heads and, where the water has receded, there is deadened gray strip. Earlier the tules were such a deep green that they looked almost black, beautiful in the changing sunlight and shadows. Time and my sense of season have been distorted by this cool, wet spring and summer...it feels spring-like. It seems that things should still be coming on, but the reservoir shows me that autumn is on the way.

Down to the causeway for a closer look. Thirty-some Killdeer on the near mud-flat...feeding, preening. Now there's the hint of a breeze. It carries the scent of swamp as it always does at summer's end. A film of greenish algae is on the water's surface. It's obvious where the water is more open, but it extends back into the dense vegetation...as far as I can see. Less than pretty to my human eye, but a pair of Green-winged Teal are scooping it up with relish. Life's all a matter of perspective.

Drive on to the east end. More birds and here are some of our Western Grebes...two are moving toward the roadway...and three young with them...typical swan-like silhouette of the Grebe but all soft, gray plumage...delightful. I've long hoped to watch a family. Now one adult moves away, followed by two young. Can't see the third juvenile...there it is, behind the second adult. Now

it pushes under her wing...looks silly with only its rump showing and the black feet thrashing around. Out of sight under her wing. Turn up the power on the spotting scope...now her upper feathers are being ruffled...a small head appears...more struggle...and there! Atop the adult, gazing all around...must be quite a change of scenery. The adult is very quiet while the young one wiggles and squirms, and I can plainly see the typical red eye of the Grebe clan. Here comes the other adult with a 3-inch dark-looking, writhing object...offers it to the young one...slurp! Eating pretty high. I've read about such behavior for years, but now I've seen it for myself. And the family moves back toward the 6-feet-tall tules...vanished.

These 2-foot-long birds appear in late spring each year. As is the pattern of their species, they take up residence in the emerging growth of tules or cattails and their colonies may number in the hundreds. This spring I watched Grebes swim toward each other, bow, and appear to preen in stylized motions. Then they would rise up, seemingly to stand on their tails, and together race across the water with a loud rushing sound. Sometimes several or even small groups would join, all diving back into the water like synchronized dolphins. Then they'd casually swim and forage. When we fished on Lake Mead in Nevada, we'd often see whole flotillas of Western Grebes performing in this manner in winter, so it's not courtship behavior as people often assume it to be, but it is rather a social behavior, perhaps to release nervous tension. And I think of our Sandhill Cranes where the familiar "dance" is primarily a social event, as well as a prelude to the true courtship that is the unison call between a mated pair.

I've read in Fred Ryser's *Birds of the Great Basin* of the Grebe's true courtship. One bird will emerge with a beak full of water weeds. Often a second bird will do the same, and then the two may swim toward each other. They rise up from the water beak to beak, holding the potential nesting materials. They lean upon each other and then sink down slowly. This is interpreted as the true courtship behavior and is pictured in the *Birder's Handbook*. The floating nest holds three or four 2-inch eggs and, when they hatch in about three weeks, the chicks are open-eyed, downy, and can soon swim.

The main diet for Western Grebes is fish, fresh and bony. The adults are known to eat their own feathers and they feed feathers to their young. As with the Eared Grebe, a possible reason for the resulting feather balls could be to cushion the sharp bones. Another theory is that the feathers would slow the digestive action, allowing the bones to soften. If I'm more watchful, I'm sure to see this here at the Basin. And here come two more Grebes, rushing across the calm surface, with shining white breasts. During the late 1800s these birds were slaughtered for their breast feathers, which were sold as furs. The skin is tough and the feathers dense: Therefore the Grebes' skins were sold as animal pelts. Now, despite loss of habitat and poisoning by the derivatives of DDT, our Western Grebes flourish at Hart's Basin. Though there are other Grebe species worldwide, the Western is restricted to our continent.

In the spring, the Common Mergansers are early arrivals, and any white-bodied bird on our reservoir is probably a Merganser. When they start to leave, the Western Grebes begin to arrive, and some will stay to nest. So, my rule of thumb: Mergansers in late winter, Western Grebes in early spring. But now autumn approaches, and before long, our Western Grebes will be leaving for their winter quarters, perhaps as far south as central Mexico. But I know that some will return to us next spring.

Autumn

Fireweed in fruit
Epilobium angustifolium

GREAT BLUE HERON

Water's going down fast now...can't help but wonder what it will be like by summer's end. Shorebird watching at Hart's Basin is pretty much a spotting scope job now. But I can see two large gray birds at the far east end...magnification up on the spotting scope...one sitting with shoulders hunched up...the other wading slowly in the shallows, neck outstretched...like a walking statue...typical feeding pattern of the Great Blue Heron.

Down to the causeway for a closer look. I miss the song of the Blackbirds...the Redwings and Yellow-heads aren't nesting in the cattails and tules this year since there's no water under them. No water...no birds...no songs. There are two Great Blues along the inlet...more out in the weed patch...two, three...four...six. Focus on one. As tall as a Sandhill Crane and often mistaken for it. But the Crane is solitary with a ground nest while the Herons are in colonies with nests in trees and, interestingly, Herons have four toes (to grasp the limb) but Cranes only have three toes. So if you see a large gray bird in a tree, it is not a Crane, but a Heron.

The back, wings, and neck of my bird are dark gray...no, the front of the 18-inch-long neck is lighter colored with shaggy feathers hanging down...rather like those of an Egret. The whitish head is set off by a long dark plume pointed toward the back and extending well beyond the head itself. As I focus on this bird, another flies through my field of view...follow it for a ways. Slow, steady wing beat...shows the darker trailing edge of the 6-feet wing span...as big as an eagle! The neck is in the typical curve...looks almost neck-less.

Now look for a Great Blue with an all-dark head...don't see any. These would be young ones...it's a bit soon to expect them I guess, although there were over fifty nests counted in the colony by the dam. It's humorous to watch these 4-foot-tall birds  land in the treetops to nest on their broad platform of sticks. The colony seems to move about our valley: there used to be one along the river near Hotchkiss, then another by Confluence Park, and now this one by Hart's Basin that increases each year. I realize that I had best enjoy them before they decide to move again. These particular birds seem to be more or less resident, for I've seen them at the Basin in winter when there's a bit of open water, and they're regularly observed along the Gunnison River. The scientific name is interesting: *Ardea herodias*. Latin "ardea" means "heron" and Greek "erodios" means heron. Translation: heron heron. And group names for wildlife have always intrigued me: In his *Great Blue Heron*, Hayward Allen mentions that when the colony moves it's called a "siege of heron." Seems appropriate for these large birds.

It will be fun to check my references, for I know that there are five other Herons in the United States as well as more worldwide. But now the light has gone, and it's time to head for home.

STELLER'S JAY

My road passes through the broad valley of the Uncompahgre River south of Montrose. Then the valley narrows around Ridgway's Pinyon-Juniper woodlands and ahead rise the picture-book San Juan Mountains. As I approach Marian's home near Ouray, the mountains wall in my view and the road seems to vanish into the haze of the narrowing canyon. The peaks ahead are dusted with snow. Curious, spreading-twisting remnants of Fireweed's seed capsules border the roadway and occasionally their minute, cottony seeds drift by. The autumn colors of Gambel's oak and Aspen cling to the steep canyon walls of red sandstone.

Up the steep drive, around the bend, and here's the home of Rip and Marian. But before I can even step out of the car, a Steller's Jay lands upon the rock wall. The black head-crest

 works up and down, a signal of excitement. Now he flutters into a nearby Gambel's oak...the bands on the blue tail are very clear, back to the wall...preens a bit, showing the black barring on the wings. The belly fades from nearly black at the throat to a pale, sky blue, which is matched along the rump. Now down to the ground. Checks the gravel...more show than serious work...he's really looking for a handout. Up into the

Ponderosa...the white markings above the eye and under the chin shine brightly in the autumn sun. A beautiful bird. Apparently decides I'm not a "soft touch"...undulating flight down into the canyon...my bird is lost along the river vegetation.

Steller's Jay, an old friend, ranges from Alaska down the west coast and inland along the Rockies into Mexico. Its relatives comprise the Corvid Family of birds: the Ravens, Crows, and Magpies, as well as the Scrub Jay, the all-blue Pinyon Jay, the high-country Gray or Canadian Jay, and Clark's Nutcracker. Folks sometimes refer to all of the jays as "camp robbers" for their aggressive behavior but the one you're most likely to see at your camp table is the Gray or Canadian Jay. In *Colorado Birds*, Mary Taylor Gray cautions us that young birds that learn to take our handouts in summer are ill prepared to forage for natural foods when all the tourists leave, thus creating a very difficult winter season of near starvation.

A high-country resident, Steller's Jay may migrate to lower elevations during severe weather and appear at bird feeding areas. Omnivorous, they'll eat just about anything that they can find. Like many of their clan, they may store food, especially acorns and pine nuts, or steal from the caches of other birds. And they're known to take eggs and nestlings as well as insects and fruit. Their bulky nest, cemented with mud and lined with pine needles, is constructed by both parents who tend the young together. The family remains as a unit until fall.

The scientific name, *Cyanocitta stelleri*, translates as "dark blue, crested jay." For years this Sometimes-Birder thought that the bird's name was Stellar's Jay ("stellar" being associated with stars from the white facial markings). **But NO!**

It was mentioned to me by Betty and Joe Hall that the name is in honor of Georg Wilhelm Steller, the eighteenth century German naturalist who took part in Vitus Bering's Alaska expedition in 1740-1742. A sea cow, a sea lion, and an Eider (a sea duck) are also named for him. So my bird's name is "steller," with an "er" not "ar."

The Eastern Jay, expanding its range, has been reported this season on the Western Slope, so it seems that we now have all the Jays. According to the new *National Geographic Guide to North American Birds*, Steller's and the Eastern Blue Jay occasionally hybridize, so variations on the Jay theme may appear here.

Now two more Steller's Jays appear and another flies up from the river...the first bird that I saw? Much fluttering and hopping about on the deck railing...but really no contest as the two newcomers retreat to the Ponderosa and Boss-bird claims the feeder. But now my dinner awaits, and I'll leave these handsome birds to their antics.

DIPPER

To my mind, there is nothing so soothing as the gentle sound of running water. And it seems that the water's voice is quieter here since the enhancement has been completed. Though a wild stream is my delight, the ridges of rocks that have been placed across this stream seem to have benefited the fish. The rocks slow the current, creating pools that provide bits of food and resting places for the trout here in the tailwaters of the Uncompahgre River below the Ridgway Dam.

I stand upon the bridge here at Ridgway State Park's Pa-co-chu-puk fishing area, contemplating the immense quantity of water just a quarter of a mile away, behind the earthen dam that blocks my view. But I know that, just beyond, the jagged San Juan Mountains reach to the clear blue sky. And today they're decorated with the season's first dusting of snow...I feel the chill of the air and realize that summer's over, no matter the calendar date.

Allen has taken the stream's right-hand trail to try out his new fly rod and the left-hand bank appears to be unpeopled. The quiet, the gentle stream sounds, the occasional flitting of birds...what a wondrous place to be. Around one bend, then another. No human sound but my own feet on the path. And just ahead is a likely spot for birds. The stream divides here, with the main portion going beyond the little island and a quieter channel just before me.

I hear a White-Crowned Sparrow...there's a wren sound... Raven squawks overhead. Watch the water. Perfect setting for a

Dipper. And watch some more...there, at the head of the bend in the main river...a small gray bird. It hops from one rock to the next...now off the rock into the water...swift current there! It vanishes! Watch a few feet ahead of its vanishing act...there it is, foraging along and, lucky for me, it's following my channel. Into the water again...now under the water. It had a stubby silhouette...7-inches-long...almost no tail...no wing bars...nothing to note, just a gray bird.

Back again...bobbing up and down on a moss-covered rock. A continuous movement..."dipping" is the basis of its name, Dipper. Some researchers suggest this movement may be signals for the mate. It's ready to go again...and there's that flash of white in the eye. The Dipper has an extra set of eye lids, a nictitating membrane, that protects the eye when the bird's under water. Gone...start counting...it should surface in thirty seconds or less. There it is, but of course I can't make out the scales that protect its nostrils when it's underwater. The Dipper's adaptations to its stream environment are nothing short of amazing. When it goes under, the heartbeat slows and the blood is sent to the primary sites (eyes, brain, internal organs); the reverse occurs upon surfacing.

The most impossible to me is the plumage; just ordinary feathers. But the Dipper goes in and out of the icy-cold mountain stream waters as easily as a Jay flits from branch to branch. How does he do it? First, the bird possesses very large oil glands with which to waterproof its outer feathers. Then there is a very dense coat of down, for if the water penetrates to the skin, the bird would suffer, perhaps even cease to function. At first observance, it surprised me that the Dipper moved upstream, against the swift currents. But if it were otherwise, the feathers would be ruffled and the water could penetrate. Although its habitat makes study difficult, it has been found that this thrush-like bird can walk on the stream bottom or use its wings to "fly" underwater. It can function to twenty feet below the surface (so says the literature, but that couldn't apply to our small western streams). And it can forage in water too deep and swift for a human to manage (to that I can attest!).

Though this 2-ounce bird appears to be resident, there is usually an altitudinal migration with high-country birds appearing at lower sites such as this stream. However, some may winter as far south as Central America. These birds consume small fish, aquatic insects, and vegetation. The habitat of swift, clear water is the same for trout as it is for Dipper. So, there it is, a need for cooperation between birders and fishermen.

The bird hesitates in a quiet pool across the channel. There's a bit of quieter water between a fallen log and the rocky shore...a good nest site? I'd dearly love to see the ball of moss that serves as a nest. It's likened to a Dutch-oven with an entrance down in front. And the preferred site is cooled by spray, or even behind a waterfall.

Perhaps next spring we can visit here at Ridgway State Park and walk this path. Perhaps I'll spot a Dipper's nest.

EASTERN BLUE JAY

The famous Blue Jay of eastern North America, known for its noisy calling and its aggressive behavior, is expanding its range westward. It's listed as a "casual visitor" (irregularly appearing) in the northwest and in the Great Basin (Utah and Nevada). According to Mary Taylor Gray's *Colorado Birds*, it was first seen in Colorado in 1903 but has now become established in eastern Colorado and along the urban corridor. As we alter the landscape by fragmenting the forests and creating residential areas, we create suitable habitat for this handsome bird.

During the winter of 1998-99, a Blue Jay appeared in Hotchkiss at the feeders of Marilyn Tate. Although she called me, the bird and I never quite made contact. Now Marilyn has provided a backyard photo of this eastern wanderer, busily  eating near her birdbath. The facial markings are distinct: white with dark necklace and eye streak plus an obvious crest. The basic color is, of course, blue. The breast and belly are white, and there are also white markings within the wings and bordering the barred tail. The only other crested Jay, our high-country Steller's, is dark overall with only a few white streaks about the face. According to the *Birder's Handbook*, these two may interbreed where their ranges overlap along Colorado's Front Range but little study seems to have been done. So, something to watch for.

It's interesting to note some of the bird's habits. It's known to cache food and, although it's notorious for nest raiding, it also eats small mammals, insects, and carrion with a primary diet of acorns, fruits, and seeds. Both parents build the nest, incubate the four or five eggs for about two weeks, and tend the young until they fly in about three more weeks. The parents may aggressively chase away owls during nesting. Gregarious, these birds may migrate in large flocks and are often scolded or mobbed by smaller songbirds. They're certainly not songsters but, interestingly, they are able to mimic the cry of the Red-shouldered Hawk, which occurs within their range.

The term "jay" may have been a Roman pet-name or come from "gay," referring to the bright plumage. Properly, our bird is labeled *Cyanocitta cristata* (Greek "kuanos" for dark, plus "kitta" for jay and Latin "cristata" for crest). The Blue Jay is a member of the Corvid Family of birds, which includes Ravens and Crows, Magpies and all of the Jays. The Corvids, as a Family, are gregarious and noisy so that we notice them before we notice others birds. Although many bird species readily take the eggs and nestlings of other birds, we may not notice them but we surely do notice the Corvids.

In our eastern states, there are only two Jays. The Gray or Canadian Jay occurs there, but it also occurs through the Rocky Mountains and into Colorado. And, of course, there's the Eastern Blue Jay, but now it's been photographed here on the Western Slope, too. In addition, there have been reports of the Gray-breasted or Mexican Jay (of our southwestern deserts). So, it seems that we may have them all: Eastern, Steller's, Gray, Scrub, Pinyon, plus Clark's Nutcracker. Pretty good birding!

MAGPIE

Against the backdrop of the hazy slopes of Grand Mesa, my eye follows the undulating flight of a Magpie...little else moves. The usual crowds of small birds that have visited us every year seem to have vanished. The flock of Red-winged Blackbirds now numbers a mere half dozen...only a few of the colorful House Finches sip from the watering dish and I haven't seen a Gold Finch for weeks. Before this season, drought was only a word in the dictionary to me, but now I'm beginning to understand the true meaning.

My Magpie approaches our yard only to turn west by Stuart's barn across the road...out of sight, but I know what it's doing, for Stuart leaves food out for the birds. Now out from behind the garage...all black and white...hopping-walking along.

 They hoard food just as do the other members of the Corvid Family of birds that includes all the Crows, Ravens, Jays, and Clark's Nutcracker. We have this entire group on the Western Slope, except for the Eastern Blue Jay, and it has been sighted in Hotchkiss and Delta. Here's a second Magpie foraging along...most likely a pair, since they form a long-term pair-bond and remain together throughout the year.

On the causeway several seasons ago, I met a gentleman from Boston who was thrilled to see a Magpie: It was a "life bird" for him. I'd never given much thought to this common, resident bird, and I recall checking the field guide (it's not listed for the northeast!). Intrigued, I turned to my references when I reached home and found a wealth of information. Hal Harrison, in his *Field Guide to Western Birds' Nests*, describes the nest: It consists of an inner bowl, nearly a foot in diameter, constructed of mud or cow dung. Over this the birds build a canopy of interlacing twigs and sticks, often thorny ones. The entire nest is usually about 3-feet-high and equally broad. It may take over a month to construct and is often utilized later by other birds and even mammals. There is an obscure main entrance on one side with an escape exit on the other side. Such nests are a familiar sight in our area in thorny shrubs or tall trees.

Now the Magpies fly up into the orchard trees right across the road...then onto the fence...their plumage a beautiful iridescent greenish-purple in the dull sunlight. They both try to balance on the narrow wire...leaning this way and that, swaying back and forth. Such a long tail is a hazard, even when it's not a windy day. Though the primary diet of these omnivorous birds is insects and carrion, they'll take seeds, fruits, and just about anything they can find. And, like many other birds, they're not above nest robbing. Known for their intelligence, it's been recorded that they will follow predators, such as coyotes, in hopes of snatching a scrap or two. In her *Bird Brains*, Candace Savage discusses the intelligence of Crows, Ravens, Magpies, and Jays and gives an overview of the world's Corvids or Crow Family. Beautiful color photography plus the most recent research findings create delightful reading to anyone interested in birds.

Though not always welcome and often shot at as "varmints" and fair game for target practice, these noisy, 20-inch-long birds are frequently near human habitations where there's often food to be found. Research has it that about seventy percent of their diet is insects and such: useful birds. And now in this year of drought, the Magpies will survive.

Along the
Migration Route

MIGRATION ROUTE

Since my first encounter with the Greater Sandhill Cranes, I've been enamored with these magnificent birds. I want to know everything that I can about them, and this has resulted in a new passion during my retirement years. During Crane Season, phone messages from people in the Delta area have led to a better understanding of the movements of the birds, and Melvin Peterson graciously shared his knowledge gained during the Cross-fostering Project (aimed at establishing a migratory group of Whooping Cranes within this flock of Sandhills). To keep tabs on the endangered Whooping Cranes, the flock was monitored by aircraft, so their migration route is well defined.

My earlier, simplistic understanding had the Cranes acting in unison, not only at their wintering grounds at the Bosque but through their 800-mile migration and on to the nesting grounds. Now I realize that most of them winter at the Bosque del Apache National Wildlife Refuge (some ninety miles south of Albuquerque, New Mexico), but some winter at various other sites in that region. In early February, they leave the Bosque area in groups of a few to hundreds over several weeks' time, traveling north into a staging area in Colorado's San Luis Valley. By late February or early March, most of the flock crosses the mountains in the region of North Pass and Cochetopa Pass near Gunnison. Then many of them come for their one-night stay at Hart's Basin. Each evening, a new group arrives only to leave us the next morning. This means that over a period of about four weeks, we usually have a daily arrival and departure, so that about half to three-quarters of the entire flock stops here at the Basin. Clearly some rest elsewhere. The next major resting area beyond us would be the Ouray NWR near Vernal, Utah.

Then the Cranes travel on to their nesting grounds not only around Grays Lake in Idaho, but throughout a broad band of territory that includes Colorado, Utah, Wyoming, Idaho, and points north. Those investigations must wait for another summer.

When the Cranes are at the Bosque or in the San Luis Valley, their daily flight is from the roost to a feeding area. It is a horizontal pattern, from point A to point B. Thus, viewing them is watching a low flight or, when they land on the ground, looking through the flock. But when they land at Hart's Basin, they come from high above after a day's flight that crosses mountain passes at about 10,000 feet elevation. During their stay here, we look down at them from our hilltop as they forage in the pasture and along the reservoir's shores. And when they take off in the morning, they must gain altitude to cross more mountains, again at about 10,000 feet. So, the pattern of flight here is vertical in contrast to the horizontal flight pattern in other areas.

Furthermore, after these gregarious Cranes leave our area, their social needs are reversed. The flock dissipates into solitary mated pairs, intent on nesting and raising an offspring. Though unmated juveniles may remain together for a while, the flock as such has served its purpose. Now the mated pairs require solitude, space, and sufficient resources. This is not a time for people-viewing. So the places and times for viewing are at the Bosque, the San Luis Valley, and Hart's Basin.

In following their migration route, we begin here at home near the reservoir. Then we drive (since we can't fly) to Crawford, where the Cranes sometimes rest. Then on to Gunnison. From there we travel over Cochetopa Pass and down to Saguache at the upper end of the San Luis Valley. On down the valley and to the wildlife refuges at Russell Lakes, Alamosa, and Monte Vista to finally arrive at the Bosque itself. A fascinating journey.

WILSON'S WARBLER

We're on Highway 92, a familiar road that we've often traveled in following the migration route of our Sandhill Cranes. Since our bed is secured for tonight (we've made a reservation in Gunnison), we have a bit of time to stop and enjoy Crawford Reservoir. From the turnout along the west shore road, I can see plenty of birds...Coots, Canada Geese, and a variety of ducks in their dull, non-breeding, or eclipse plumage. Years ago, on a cold spring day, I saw this shore lined with Sandhill Cranes. A sight that I'll never forget.

But now we go farther along on this westside road to a parking space for fishermen. It's less used than the highway side with its modern camping sites, so my chances of finding birds (and Allen's of finding fish) are often better here. I plan to walk the little used trail along the shoreline toward the south. Here I find skunkbush, willows, and cottonwoods nearer the water with juniper and pinyon upslope. All likely cover for small songbirds such as sparrows, warblers, and flycatchers. Now I find a bit of shade and sit quietly...I hear the "buzzy" note of a wren...there, on a juniper branch. It moves around...visible now...brown back and underside all white. There's the distinctive white eye-line...and white along the edges of the upright tail...so it's Bewick's Wren. An ongoing frustration surfaces again. This little charmer was named for Thomas Bewick, late 1700s, and I've heard it pronounced like the car, "Buick." But I've never found justification for that pronunciation...I'd like to have a time machine so that I could go back and ask the gentleman himself to pronounce his name! But my Wren is upset with my presence, so I'll move on.

Now back past the car, through the gate, and walk along the Indian Fire Nature Trail. The slopes above are pinyon and juniper at the top, then comes wild rose and currant. The vegetation comes in layers: near the bottom are willows, then tules, then cattails, and finally dense undergrowth. The quantity of vegetation is amazing, considering the small amount of water available in this narrow ravine. This is excellent cover for a whole variety of birds...water means life in our arid region.

Stand quietly and wait. A flash of yellow...no markings that I  could catch. I was told that if I should see small birds (4 or 5 inches long) that flit through the cover faster than I can focus my binoculars, they're likely "warblers." That fits this bird, so I'll guess "warbler." Ah, there it is again...an all-yellow bird with a conspicuous dark eye in the yellow face. But there! Now I see that it has a black crown...Wilson's Warbler! It's been a while since I've seen this bird. I recall that when I first became interested in watching birds, I attended a lecture/field trip at the University in Las Vegas...that goes back a ways. I'd seen a bright yellow bird with a black cap during a Utah fishing trip, and Dr. Bepler said that it was likely a Wilson's Warbler. Now I've seen it at several mountain sites.

I know that its nesting grounds reach far into the forests of Alaska and Canada, as well as southward through the Rocky Mountains, and that willow thickets such as this one are a favored nesting place. My little 4-inch bird goes off, flitting among the leaves. It seems to be still for a moment...no, it's sort of bouncing up and down. It appears to be picking something off the leaf above its head. What a neat trick! But tough to be a bug. Now it's off again... but the movement is purposeful...no doubt catching insects much too small for me to see.

I walk up the other side of the ravine and find a handy stone bench. It's littered with emptied seed heads from sunflowers and rabbitbrush...a convenient table for chipmunk and squirrel. It's a lovely view from here: juniper woodland downslope, then the willows and a couple of boats on the reservoir. The highway seems to be far away right now and the distant hills, ever increasing in height to become the mountains surrounding the Needle Rock formation, are sharp with shadows and low sunlight. Ah, perfect...a soaring Redtail Hawk high over the blue water. This is a peaceful place and an interesting trail. Perhaps we can stop here on our way back home.

COMMON NIGHTHAWK

Another stop along our Sandhill Cranes' migration route. We've stayed over here in Gunnison and now, before it gets dark, I have time to look for birds along this channel of the Gunnison River. A clear, calm evening and the birds are very active...Swallows are everywhere...a couple of Robins nearby, Grackles and Brown-headed Cowbirds under the bird feeders across the way. Hummingbirds zipping by and a Yellow Warbler

in the willows. A productive site. There's a bird call behind me...one note with a muffled quality to it, and there's a Common Nighthawk swooping down river. Now it's overhead and I can see the horizontal white patch against the dark wing. The Robin-sized body is slim and the wingspan is more than twice the body length...a falcon-like shape with the tail widened at the tip rather than straight. It goes on down the river...back toward me again. The tip of the tail is black, then there's a white band...then narrow, dark bands continue up through the body and inner portions of the wings. Now there are several more Nighthawks...darting...like bats. The white chin stripe is obvious. In the evening or at dawn and sometimes on cloudy days, these large-mouthed birds appear to scoop up flying insects. I wonder how they feed on rainy evenings. Maybe that's when they glean insects on the ground or from the foliage...a behavior that I'd like to observe.

These grayish-brown Nighthawks are not hawk-like at all, sweeping erratically back and forth in the twilight. Ouch...annoying mosquitoes! There is lots of bug activity as well bird activity! Stand still and watch...clouds of tiny insects ahead near the willows...more over the river itself. These are the Nighthawks' food source. So the seemingly erratic flight of these birds is not erratic at all, just part of the chase. It's rather like baleen whales who swim through the water with their mouths open, and the baleen sifts out the edible bits. So my birds fly with their mouths open, and clamp down on edible bits; so the Creole name fits: "crapaud volant," meaning "flying frog."

During courtship, the male Nighthawk dives straight down toward the female, pulling upward only at the very last moment. As he halts his dive, he claps his strong wings downward so that the primary feathers vibrate, creating the sound that seems to some to be like the bellowing of a bull: so, came the old vernacular name of "bullbat."

These insect eaters nest throughout the North American continent and winter in South America as far south as Northern Argentina. The female doesn't bother building a nest; instead, she lays her two eggs on the ground. Though they prefer soft sand, the eggs can be found in abandoned bird nests, on bare stumps, and on gravel roofs. During the dark winter months, I recall chuckling as I read that Nighthawks became common in cities with the advent of flat, gravel rooftops...just have to make-do! The female does most of the incubating for about twenty days. Then both the male and the female tend the young, feeding them regurgitant. The young fly within twenty-one days and are able to feed themselves by the twenty-fifth day.

Most birds perch on a branch cross wise, but one of the unusual behaviors of Nighthawks is to sit "length wise" on branches to roost. Several years ago, before the island across this channel of the Gunnison River was developed into RV sites, I spotted a Common Nighthawk at roost. At first it looked like a lump or swelling along the branch. It was so well camouflaged that I'd have missed it if Arlie hadn't shown me exactly where to look.

Names reflect our attempts to organize our world, and our bird is *Chordeiles minor* which translates from the Greek as "choreia" (dancing) and "deiles" (evening), so our Nighthawks dance in the evening. That fits. But "minor?" It turns out that our bird was about 1-inch smaller than the only other known such bird, the European Nightjar. Another puzzle: Our birds are also members of the Goatsucker group. I wondered about that for years. Since these birds are insect eaters, they may feed on insects stirred up by animals and are thereby often found near livestock. Because they are nocturnal, it was apparently assumed that they were damaging in some way. So it was believed that they sucked the goats' milk at night, hence the common name "goatsucker." The Latin "caper" (goat) and "mulgere" (to milk) gives us the scientific name of *Caprimulgus* for the genus, which includes two European species plus our American southeastern Whip-Poor-Will, the southwestern Common Poorwill, and the Texas Pauraque. These common names derive from the birds' calls. From these "jarring" noises at night, comes the term "nightjars" for the whole group. Perhaps such beliefs seem amusing, but then I have a good flashlight to explore at night, not a fitful, smoky torch.

No doubt I saw the slow flying Lesser Nighthawk in our Southwest deserts but didn't realize much about birds back then. Now there are several Nighthawks silhouetted against the sky above the river...it's almost dark. But there's one near the campsite light by the bridge. To my eye, it appears that the bird drops one wing straight down while flapping the other...the wings are working independently! Like a human rowing a boat, the left wing is working as a temporary keel while the right wing gives momentum or spin and Zap! Gone is one hapless bug. Or am I just seeing what I have been hoping to see after reading M. R. Montgomery's description in *Many Rivers to Cross?*

It's dark now. Bedtime, for we'll go on to Cochetopa Pass tomorrow. No moon tonight. I carefully walk back behind the cabin, look up, and find a sky filled with brilliant stars. A privilege these days.

COCHETOPA PASS

To reach this area, follow U.S. 50 east out of Gunnison for about eight miles. Then turn right onto State Highway 114, going south toward Saguache. This paved road follows Cochetopa Creek. It's slow going up the twisting canyon, but I find the geology interesting, and once we were fortunate to see a small group of six mountain sheep. The hay meadows and roadsides provide a display of wildflowers: Golden Banner, Lupine in blues and purples, Larkspur and the less common Purple Lousewort.

The small stream, sometimes meandering quietly through hay meadows, can become white water as it charges through the rocky curves and steep cliffs of the canyon. Here I always watch for the lovely white blossoms of our western dogwood and elderberry. The tangled streamside growth includes currant, willows, and a host of small wildflowers. The variety of trees is indicative of the climb in elevation: As we enter the canyon, Utah juniper is dominant, then Douglas fir mixed with Aspen and finally, near the upper reaches of the canyon, Engelmann's spruce appears.

Coming out of the canyon, we are in a seemingly flat region surrounded by low mountains with the high peaks of the San Juan Mountains in the distance. Closer, to the south, is the La Garita Wilderness Area with 14,000' San Luis Peak, the source of Cochetopa Creek. The rolling hills are covered with a low-growing sagebrush and the few wildflowers to be found are short: clearly a region of winds. We could continue on this paved road to North Pass, but we've discovered a back road (always preferable). About twenty-seven miles after we've turned onto State Highway 114, a dirt road goes off on the left (county road #NN14). This accesses the roads to the Old Indian Agency (built in the mid 1870s) and to Los Pinos Creek. But remaining on NN14 takes us to the fishing easements on the Coleman Ranch along Cochetopa Creek, one of our favorite fishing spots.

The area doesn't seem extraordinary: just rolling hills with distant mountains. But it is a caldera: when a volcano erupts, the expelled material leaves an empty space beneath. Of course, the earth around the volcano falls into the emptied area and creates a low spot. Then erosion from the mountains and the volcano itself fill in the area. I understand that Cochetopa Dome (11,132') is the remnant of the ancient volcano.

There is a book or ten of human history in this area. With the receding of the Pleistocene ice sheets, the area was used by humans as a north-south passage. The Paleo-Indians and the Utes came here for hunting and gathering. In fact, the name "cochetopa" means "Pass of the buffalo" in the Ute language. But for me, one of the prime interests of this area is the passageway of our Sandhill Cranes. From their staging area in the San Luis Valley, they must cross the mountains encompassed by the Rio Grande National Forest. During the Cross-fostering Project (an attempt to create a second migratory flock of the endangered Whooping Crane within our Sandhill flock), the birds were tracked by air, and many crossed in the vicinity of North Pass and Cochetopa. Likely they'd been taking that route for many centuries.

So we drive the few miles up to the summit of Cochetopa Pass. Now I have a real problem: I'm thinking about Cranes but the botany, my first love, cannot be restrained. As we begin the climb up the pass, Bristlecone pines (*Pinus aristata*) are scattered across the steep slopes. These trees grow under the

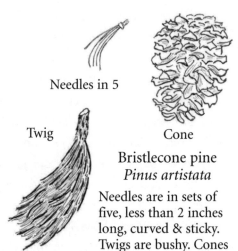

Needles in 5

Twig

Cone

Bristlecone pine
Pinus artistata

Needles are in sets of five, less than 2 inches long, curved & sticky. Twigs are bushy. Cones are bristly.

most adverse of conditions: dry, windswept slopes at high elevations. It is difficult to manage in such a harsh habitat. The twisted, gnarled limbs are covered with 2-inch curved, resinous needles, clustered along most of the twigs' length, giving it a bristly look and the common name of Fox-tail pine. The cones have unique bristles at the tip of the cone-scales. The tree's near relative, the Western bristlecone (*Pinus longaeva*) is the famous Bristlecone of the Great Basin to our west; the oldest tree yet examined (Wheeler Peak, 1964) was estimated to be 4,900 years. But our Colorado Bristlecone only lives about 400 years. Through a vast span of years, these trees are attacked by lightning, fire, disease, and erosion that removes the soils beneath their roots. But they survive. In his *Trees of the Great Basin*, Ronald Lanner suggests that perhaps it isn't that the trees live so long, but rather that they die so slowly.

The Bristlecones reproduce by seed, but their winged seeds are small, and have difficulty germinating in the brief, cold growing season. Enter the Clark's Nutcracker. This high-country pine-seed eater caches the seeds of the pine trees, including those of the bristlecone. The bird buries the seeds a couple of inches below the forest litter and the difference is dramatic. Looking upslope there are rarely single trees, most are in groups: the germinated seeds of a neglected Nutcracker's cache.

But in this extraordinary world of trees, we drive into a mix of aspen, Ponderosa pine, and Douglas fir. They should be *below* Bristlecone! But when we reach the summit at 10,067', we are in a

Cone

Needles

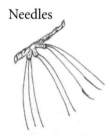

Ponderosa pine
Pinus ponderosa

Long needles in sets of two or three. No bristles on the cone.

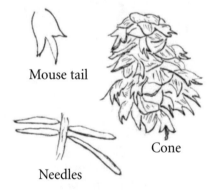

Mouse tail

Cone

Needles

Douglas fir
Pseudotsuga douglasii

A scale (called a mouse tail) extends out of the cone. Twig with flat needles that occur singly.

mix of Douglas fir, aspen, and Engelmann's spruce. Ordinarily, these trees could be sorted out by species and Life-Zone or elevation. But not here. The mix seems impossible, and it's marvelous for this amateur botanist. I walk the forest floor, finding a whole world of high-country herbaceous plants as well. I'm in ecstasy.

Aspen
Populus tremuloides

The Aspen leaves rustle in the breeze. In my mind's eye, I see barren Aspen bending in a cold wind. A crust of frozen snow. The forest is silent. And from above come the calls of the Sandhill Cranes as they traverse this "low" mountain pass. They'll fly over Gunnison and most likely over Crawford Reservoir. Some of them, we'd hope, would choose to spend the night at Hart's Basin.

A butterfly floats leisurely by, the Douglas fir and the Engelmann's spruce sigh in the gentle breeze. But, I want to stop by the Limber pine (*Pinus flexilis*) that I found last year toward the bottom of the pass. I've spent years hunting that one! So, for now, we'll leave this wondrous place of mixed-up trees and imagined Crane calls. But we'll return again.

Needles in 5

Limber pine
Pinus flexilis

Needles in sets of five, over 2 inches. Cone without bristles. Not sticky.

SAY'S PHOEBE

The world changes dramatically as we come down Cochetopa Pass into an area of rolling hills, thickly clothed with small tufts of high-country sagebrush. Erosion has played a big role in shaping this landscape: shallow gullies, dry arroyos, and steep-walled canyons. Some of the canyon walls look volcanic...but that's another whole world of study.

Now Saguache Creek makes its claim, its banks marked by dense stands of willows. The highway, of course, follows the creek's meandering course and now the valley opens out into hay meadows filled with wild iris. This breathtaking beauty has led us here on pilgrimages for many springs. This Iris, *Iris missouriensis*, is the only one native to our area, although sometimes cultivars naturalize and make their way into wildflower guides. The structure is more complex than meets the eye, and I recall growing weary after reading two pages of varieties in *Hortus Third* (a dictionary of cultivated plants). I know that other species occur worldwide in temperate zones, especially in Africa, and that the names and usages are as complex as the plants. But this time, we are here only to enjoy their beauty. Some future winter days will be devoted to the technicalities and preparing a column for the *Delta County Independent*.

Miles and miles of Iris through this valley, but I never tire of these scenes. The light is quite poor, but we'd still like to try to get some pictures. We round a bend and there is a familiar dirt road off to the left. We take it for a short distance and pull off. The flower fragrance is carried on the slight breeze. And there's a bird call. A single descending whistle. Scan the sky...no birds. Check the roofs of the tumble-down sheds...then along the fence line. My bird drifts toward an old wooden fence post and lands less than twenty feet from us. Not shy at all. It's smaller than a Robin...I'd guess about 6-inches-long. It's off again, flying low over the iris-filled pasture...back to its post...off again and back...fly-catcher behavior. The back and wings are darkish...the breast has a pretty peach-colored wash...now the long tail moves leisurely up and down...I never used to think of birds "wagging" their tails, but it's a good clue for Say's Phoebe.

This friendly flycatcher of western North America tolerates humans, and so its habits are known to many people, such as the one that nested on the cross bar of Bob and Martha's deck. It seems that a mere canopy of leaves is inadequate for this lovely bird: It wants a solid roof, and I recall one that built its nest atop a light fixture under the eaves of the science building at the university in Las Vegas.

My bird is much too busy to be disturbed by our presence. And as I watch, it forays out across the Iris. I wonder about the chicks...possibly somewhere inside the tumble-down shed. The male, female, and juveniles all look alike, so I'm not sure which I'm looking at. The female incubates the four or five inch-long eggs for a couple of weeks, and then both adults tend the young who fly within fifteen or so days.

It was interesting to read that these birds regurgitate pellets (like an owl does). Their primary food is insects, and the indigestible parts are ejected rather than allowed to travel through their digestive tract. And names fascinate me: Why Phoebe? Two stories. The name is pronounced /fee bee/, and the Greek combination of the letters "oe" sounds like our English "long e" giving credibility to the bird being named Phoebe, an alternate name for the Greek goddess Diana. Or perhaps, the name is merely ono-matopoeic (an imitation of the bird's call). Take your choice. It's a lovely bird by any name.

Say's Phoebe was named in honor of Thomas Say (mid-1800s) who served as the naturalist on Major Stephen Long's expedition to the Rocky Mountains. Say was a pioneer in ornithology and also authored a three-volume work, *American Entomology on North America*. The bird's name is *Sayornis saya*. "Ornis" is "bird" in Greek. Both terms, "Say" and "saya" are

Rocky Mountain Iris
Iris missouriensis

for Thomas Say, so the proper name is a double honorarium. The genus of *Sayornis* includes the Eastern Phoebe (a gray bird with a grayish-white breast), and the Black Phoebe that I met in Nevada. It's plumage is a striking black with a bright white breast and a white margined tail.

Interestingly, Say was a contemporary of James Audubon, who happened onto a nest of Say's Phoebes. Audubon put a silver thread on the young birds' legs and, happily, those young returned to his area the next season. This is often acknowledged as the first try at banding birds, a technique of great value in our efforts to understand their world.

I could stay right here and admire my Say's Phoebe and his beautiful world, but we must head for Saguache and then on to Monte Vista to spend the night.

SAGUACHE

The low vegetation along the road speaks of a windy, arid region. But trees lie ahead, and we reach the familiar fork in the road. Colorado State Highway 114 ends here at it's junction with U.S. Highway 285. A turn to the right leads to Monte Vista. Straight ahead leads into the town of Saguache. Going through Saguache would take us to Poncha Springs, and eventually to Buena Vista and Leadville.

But first a stop at the little restaurant. Several years ago, the waitress here told us that the town's name, pronounced /su watch/, is a Ute word meaning "water at the blue earth." A nice name but a bit of a puzzle in this high desert. The town lies at the northern end of the San Luis Valley, which qualifies as a true desert with less than 8-inches annual precipitation. It's known as North America's highest, largest mountain desert. Elevation, about 8,000 feet. So where's the water? In the mountains, of course. On the northeast rise the Sangre de Cristo Mountains and on the southwest are the San Juans, both including 14,000-foot peaks. The winter snows and summer rains drain down into this valley to form artesian wells and springs. Thus the valley before us is a land of ephemeral lakes, wetlands, and thereby wildlife, especially birds.

Summer temperatures are in the 70s. The winters, at 8,000 feet, obviously could be severe and windy. But this quiet place has attracted artists: photographers, potters, weavers, writers, and even basket makers. The major economy is ranching with cattle and sheep, all relying on the underground water.

And Saguache is just as one would expect a small western ranching town to be: the courthouse is here, a sheriff's department, elementary and high schools, grocery store, service stations, a medical clinic, and a weekly newspaper. The Pioneer Museum has seven rooms plus the jail where Alferd Packer, the "man eater," had a private cell. This incident involved Packer and a Utah mining group in the 1870s. A small party from the group went into the San Juan Mountains but did not return. Early that spring a search team set out but, unknown to them, Packer had shown up alone at the Los Pinos Indian Agency. He was looking fine and had money to spend. His story about the other five men changed several times and, in 1894, the missing men's camp was found near Slumgullion Pass, about two miles from Lake City. The prosecution claimed that Packer had murdered the men and then ate them. Packer said that he had not killed the others, except for one in self-defense, but supposedly admitted that he had eaten human flesh. So, the title "San Juan Cannibal." He was jailed in Saguache but escaped to Wyoming, only to be recaptured nine years later. Then he was tried and sentenced to hang, but the sentence was later reduced to manslaughter and Packer was sentenced to forty years in prison. But through the efforts of others, he was paroled in 1901 and finally died in Denver of natural causes in 1907. Quite a story with several versions. And there's a good deal of western history here of a more ordinary sort. But Monte Vista, and our night's rest, lies many miles down Highway 285.

RIFT VALLEY: THE SAN LUIS

Driving south on U. S. Highway 285, we gradually move away from the mountains of the Rio Grande National Forest on our right. And the valley on our left grows wider and wider. The Sangre de Cristo Mountains seem farther and farther away. What a vast expanse of little or nothing. The emptiness of high desert, so unpleasant to some but so pleasing to me. This road runs as straight as can be and, according to our road map, Colorado State Highway 17, over ten miles to the east, nearly parallels our road.

Familiar country, but now it has a new dimension for me. I've long understood that rivers frequently flow where there is an easier course that was often created by a fault. Thus the river creates a valley, and we humans follow the river's course. But the San Luis Creek runs, more or less, southeast into the San Luis Lakes just south of the Great Sand Dunes. A glance at the map makes it clear that this small stream probably didn't have much to do with the creation of this valley.

I've often wondered about this broad valley, especially when I scan the distance and find the Great Sand Dunes at the base of the Sangre de Cristos. Now I've learned that this whole area is a rift. It's part of what's called the "Rio Grande Rift" that began about 29 million years ago, geologically young. A rift is an area that is weakened for various reasons and then spreads apart. It's difficult to think of the solid earth "stretching," but that is what the evidence indicates. To the west, the crust of the Colorado Plateau is about 28 miles thick. To the east, under the Great Plains, the crust has been measured at about 31miles, but in this rift area the crust is approximately 22 miles thick. I've read of the Great Rift on the African continent and that there's one under the Pacific Ocean, but the concept seemed remote. Until now.

This rift starts in the Rockies near Leadville and runs south through Colorado, New Mexico, and into the state of Chihuahua in Mexico. Such earth movement is accompanied by faulting with the related earthquakes and by volcanic activities. The rift can be viewed now as four joined basins labeled the Upper Arkansas, the San Luis, Espanola, and Albuquerque. And the San Luis Basin, about 45 miles wide and 100 miles long, has been filled with sediment from the Sangre de Cristos to a depth of nearly 4 miles. A lot of erosion. A lot of years. Beyond my human reckoning. As a society, we don't blink at millions or billions or trillions of dollars of debt. But I've no real concept of such numbers.

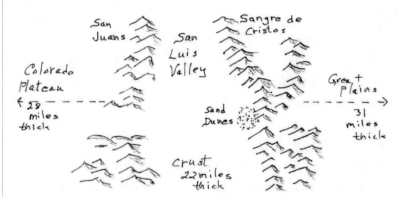

The winds blew from the southwest carrying the rift-valley's sediments until they met the Sangre de Cristos, where the heavier sand was left at the mountains' base. Result: sand dunes. They stand over 700 feet above the valley floor at over 8,000 feet elevation and cover approximately 40 square miles. A marvelous world that I long to explore.

And, of course, the water. Its story begins in the high mountain peaks, supplemented by the scant precipitation. As this precious liquid seeps down through rock and sediment, it forms layers of water defined as various kinds of aquifers. Sometimes the underground water surfaces to form the ephemeral lakes and wetlands so crucial to wildlife utilizing this natural highway. So the fact of the migration of our Sandhill Cranes becomes eminently reasonable. They've been on the planet much longer than we have.

But plentiful water is not necessarily the only ingredient in successful agriculture. The water often lies close to the surface and excessive surface watering (irrigation) has led to water logging. Water-logged soils become alkaline and saline. And the high elevation also means lower temperatures, so the growing season is very short, suitable for hay and potatoes in the north plus cool-weather crops such as lettuce and spinach in the south around Alamosa. But there's a down side. In this era of population explosion, there are many who covet this underground water that apparently seems to them to be surplus, wasted, not used. Yet.

And this valley abounds with human history as well. Coronado may have passed this way in 1541 in search of the seven cities of gold. Then, around 1680, LaSalle proclaimed all the territory east of the Rockies for France. In the 1700s and early 1800s, various seekers and explorers passed through the area. Mexico granted lands to wealthy patrons, hoping to forestall the claims of the United States and of Texas (an impendent republic at that time). Fremont came through the region. The Louisiana Purchase, Mexico's yielding of its claims, and the purchase of Texas claims finally resulted in Colorado's boundaries. In 1851 the town of San Luis was founded (the oldest Colorado town) along with Fort Massachusetts (established to protect the town from Indian raids). Of course, San Luis is equivalent to Saint Louis: seems odd to have one in Colorado and the other in Missouri. The first newspaper, the first school, the first church: all are given in the town's website.

But for this writer, a moment of great note was the creation of the National Wildlife Refuge System and the establishment of the Bosque del Apache as well as the Alamosa/Monte Vista Refuges. These support and provide for the creatures, including the birds, that rely upon these places for their survival. And upon our willingness to protect and expand these efforts.

GREASEWOOD-FLAT PELICANS

In years past, we've stopped here at Russell Lakes about ten miles south of Saguache. Like so much of the San Luis Valley, its appearance is deceiving. This State Wildlife Refuge isn't shown on most maps and it's not organized for people activities. Most of it is closed from March or so until July to provide undisturbed habitat for our nesting birds. This area is really for the birds. Dandy with us.

We turn off on one of the dirt side roads and drive through the greasewood flats. Beyond the rickety barbed-wire fence, the landscape is in shades of greens: greasewood and sagebrush, tules and cattails. Occasionally we get a glimpse of a watery sheen, but no real, visible water. We agree to turn around. But there's something white moving through the vegetation. We stop to investigate.

Pelicans! Three of them drifting along through the greasewood. What a weird sight! They seem calm enough...I get out of the car...from this slightly higher viewpoint, I can guess at the water beneath the birds. Drive up a ways where the road's a bit higher and we can see the wake of their big yellow feet in the shallow water...it couldn't be but a few inches deep. They could easily walk, but it's probably more comfortable to putz along like this. One has the flap on its bill that is the Pelican's version of breeding plumage. One looks younger with darkish feathers down the back of its neck. In fact, the entire plumage is rather dull instead of shining white, and the bill isn't the clear yellow-orange of the mature bird. But the third one...the back of the neck looks darkish...but the bill has a flap! Check it with the scope...face is white...bill yellow...back of the head and down the neck is definitely darker. A precocious Pelican? I do wonder what the relationship of these three might be.

They look docile now, but I'd certainly not want to meet one that was angry. Their wingspan, at 9-feet, is the largest on our continent. They're just over 5-feet-long and they weigh in at over 16-pounds. The adult plumage is shining white except for the black on the trailing edge of the wings. They are huge. And I recall a windy day at Blue Mesa Reservoir near Gunnison when we stopped to watch a dozen fly overhead. The strong wind didn't seem to phase them! A California tourist had also stopped to watch the birds. He was awestruck. To him "Pelican" meant the Brown Pelican of coastal regions. That one is impressive, but the wingspan is just over 6-feet and the overall brown coloring is far less spectacular than our American White Pelican.

Back about six years ago, we had a large flock of over a hundred at Hart's Basin. Then came the drought, and the water was drawn down further than usual for irrigation. Next, the dam needed repair and the water was drawn out completely. The shoreline was shingled with dead carp. But amazingly, as the reservoir filled the next season, the Great Blue Herons, the Cormorants, and a fair-sized group of Pelicans seemed to have plenty of carp to eat. But last year the reservoir was emptied again, and this spring I've seen little indication of a carp population. No food, no Pelicans. But carp are amazingly resilient. Hope.

And during the summer of 2002, the breeding colony of Pelicans at Antero Reservoir suffered greatly when that reservoir was emptied to provide water for the Front Range. But here are three Pelicans in the most unlikely setting. We watch them drift along. Then they're out of sight. They've turned and are coming back toward us. And I recall watching a small group feeding at Hart's Basin. All in a line, but then the birds on either end swam a bit faster and the group formed themselves into a "U" shape. The formation swam slowly toward the shore and then they began to feed, apparently on trapped fish. Heads down and rumps up. I could see the dark line formed by their black wingtips. Fascinating.

But I've never seen Pelicans swimming leisurely along through the greasewood. What a wonderful scene to remember in the winter days to come.

DROUGHT AND BLACK-CROWNED NIGHT-HERONS

I'd hoped to see Kelli Stone, the Refuge biologist that I correspond with by e-mail during the Crane migration, but we've missed her today. However, the volunteer at the visitors' center has been very helpful. She pointed out the severity of the drought conditions in the valley. These wetlands depend primarily upon ground water, as does the agricultural industry, and there is just not enough water to go around. She warned us that many of the wetlands would be dry and to be particularly careful not to disturb the birds who are being forced into smaller, restricted areas.

This complex includes two national wildlife refuges: one here at Alamosa and the one up the road at Monte Vista where we are staying. Here at Alamosa, a county road runs along the northern and eastern edges of the Refuge, but this offers little potential for bird-watching under such dry conditions. The volunteer suggests that we follow the Auto Tour Route, which runs west from the headquarters, then south, and circles back east-north to the headquarters.

Dry, dry, dry. Pond after pond of dried mud-cakes, bounded by tules and cattails that seem to be dying back. But today the clouds are moving in swiftly. Hope for rain. We've reached the right-angle turn on the Route and head south. There's a bit of water ahead. Slow down, turn the car at a bit of an angle for better viewing with the spotting scope out the window. Stop. Wait. There's a fair-sized bird at the water's edge...the hunched silhouette of a Heron...but much too small for Great Blue. Mount the spotting scope...it's a Black-crowned Night-heron.

Statue still, now moving to the right...out of sight. This is an old friend of Hart's Basin where they appear each summer, and I've often seen one perched along the inlet shrubs. Most of the time, they've just sat still. You wouldn't know they were there if you weren't attuned to their favored perches.

I've read that they have several styles of foraging: stand and wait, stalk, hover, plunge, and swim. But I've never been lucky enough to see any such behavior. All I've ever seen is the hunched silhouette. I know that they eat fish, insects, small mammals, and frogs, as well as the eggs and nestlings of other birds. At first, reading about such predation distressed me, but now I've come to realize that it's the rule rather than the exception in the bird world, just as it is in the animal world.

Black-crowned Night-herons nest throughout the North American continent and winter into Central and South America and, according to the literature, they especially like to winter in Cuba. These birds may build a flimsy nest, or a sturdy one. They may build the nest in trees (less than 30-feet high), in brush, or in heavy cover. There are usually five or less 2-inch-long eggs, which hatch asynchronously (at varying times), and the chicks are noisy, downy, with eyes open, and waiting to be fed. The adults feed them regurgitated food at first but soon the chicks get fresh fish. The parents stay together for the season and work together to build the nest and tend the young, who fly in about seven weeks, a long time for the adults to provide.

We move the car forward a bit and stop again. Perfect! there's my Black-crown...on a low branch...horizontal to the ground. The underside is snowy white, and there are the yellow-orange legs. The bill is long and sharp, rather thick...the red eye is conspicuous. The back is black but the wings are gray...hardly any tail at all. The bird's crown is shiny black and I can just make out the long plumes that come from the nape of his neck. This is his breeding ornamentation. What a wonderful view! But wait...something special. Here's a double-bird...a Black-crown sitting in the water...and a flawless reflection of a second bird, with drifting white plumes. Lovely.

Allen says that there are several more Black-crowns...use the binoculars for a broader view. There's one with its neck stretched up. I've never seen that! The neck is nearly as thick as the body. In field guides these birds are often pictured in flight, with the thick neck stretched out. But the few times that I've seen them in flight the neck was doubled back in typical "heron-style." This one just seems to be stretching...now the head goes back down into the hunched shoulders. We count a total of seven Black-crowns. And, over all these years, we've never seen more than one at a time.

Their proper name is *Nycticorax nycticornex*. In ancient times they were considered birds of ill omen: "nycti" means "night." And anything that was out at night was considered evil to day-oriented humans. Why night active? Competition from other creatures is an important aspect of feeding patterns. Its cousin, the Great Blue Heron, measures 46-inches and weighs over 5-pounds while the Black-crown is a mere 25-inches and weighs less than a pound. Foraging at dawn, dusk, and night is obviously a safer time.

Sadly, the storm's moved on. Seeing seven Black-crowns at once is a real treat. But it's also indicative of the stressful conditions for the wildlife in the entire area. Drought is an ugly word.

MONTE VISTA REFUGE: AVOCETS

Clear sky and bright sunshine. And we're off to explore the Monte Vista Wildlife Refuge. The Auto Tour produces little for birds. Some Red-winged Blackbirds and a few Yellow-heads in the cattails. I thought I heard a Marsh Wren but couldn't really be sure. Several Mallards and a few Cinnamon Teal. Not even many Coots. We'll soon junction with Highway 15 leading out of the Refuge.

Wind's up and the heavy clouds seem to have come from nowhere. Again, hope for rain. We stop to eat our lunch. But a bird just flew into the cattails...just ahead of us. We pull up a bit farther and there it is...perched sideways on a cattail. It's a Song Sparrow. And here's a small opening with shallow water, and out in the water is an Avocet...long blue-gray legs, white body trimmed in black with a lovely peach-colored wash down the neck and breast. Avocets are as pretty as their name.

The small area is encircled with tall cattails...sort of a mini-bay. And on the muddy strip, between the plants and the shallow bit of water, stand Avocets...a dozen of them! At home the largest number of Avocets that I've seen at one time was half a dozen, so this is really special.

Some are preening, others foraging with that peculiar side-sweeping motion, needle-thin black bills back and forth, back and forth across the skim of water. But the wind begins to rock the car. Thunder rumbles...lightning. And the Avocets all come to stand on the muddy shore in the shelter of the tall cattails.

They seem to arrange themselves in a line, at least from our perspective. Lashing rain comes down, cold and hard, and I roll up the car window. Something has disturbed the birds...just the storm? Scan the wind-lashed tules with my binoculars...don't see anything like a predator.

The Avocets all move out to the very edge of the water. How strange...they are all standing upright. I've never seen that erect posture. Allen says that they look like a bunch of Penguins...and they do. How extraordinary! The wind blows, the rain-hail mix pelts the water's surface, the cattails bend and twist. The birds stand. Endure. But suddenly they all charge into the water, scrambling away from their shelter despite the turbulent wind.

Time passes...the storm continues. Slowly, the birds begin to seek new shelter. A few move off toward the pond's far end...others begin to forage, storm or no. Some just stand in the water, in their normal horizontal posture. What a special moment we've witnessed.

BOSQUE DEL APACHE
National Wildlife Refuge

This is the culmination of the migration route for our Greater Sandhill Cranes of Hart's Basin. This is their wintering grounds, the Bosque del Apache. And in years past we've come for the Festival of Cranes whenever we could manage.

Bosque Del Apache, Fly-out

It's cold and dark here before dawn. There's a muffled rustling sound...feathers? The pond on our left appears to be white with dark splotches. Now muted sounds of disturbed water, of bird voices, of movement. The sky grows less dark in the east and a single coyote call drifts across the Refuge...another answers...more...and the solitude is filled with their morning song. The ponds on both sides of the roadway stir with birds. With the growing light, the predawn white areas are transformed into hundreds of individual Snow Geese...the dark splotches into Sandhill Cranes and uncountable ducks. The darkness slowly withdraws...the Geese stretch and preen. Their high-pitched voices grow loud, excited, and suddenly Snow Geese lift from the water...coming straight at us...I feel the rush of air from their wings as they barely clear the tops of the willows. More voices, more Geese...the ponds are lost from view as thousands lift into the air... pandemonium!

The ponds reappear...the water shimmers. The night sky to the west is obscured with white Snow Geese. But the eastern sky grows lighter...the few clouds are under-lit with delicate pinks and golds. Some of the ducks begin to forage, white rumps pointed skyward...a few take flight. The Sandhill Cranes stand one-legged, head under wing in their watery roost, safe from coyote. Now they rouse to stretch and shake their feathers, their voices muted, sleepy. The few remaining Snow Geese leave in small groups. There's enough light to distinguish the ducks' plumage...Mallard and Pintail...Gadwall and Wigeon...Shovelers and Cinnamon Teal.

Now the Sandhills consider take-off....familiar sounds of Hart's Basin. At home take-off occurs at mid-morning, for they must wait for the thermal updrafts that enable them to gain sufficient altitude to continue their migration. But here on the wintering grounds at the Bosque, the day's level flight is merely to the adjacent fields, which are prepared for them by the Refuge management. A family group of three takes flight...then another...a set of twelve or so. And then, just as the sun tops the horizon, the rest take flight. The rush of wings directly overhead, the familiar cries escalating into an impossible din. But more birds erupt from the adjacent ponds...hundreds...thousands all at once. The ponds to our left are lost in the low rays of the sun, but on the right we watch the ducks and teal take to the air as well. The sounds, the rush of air against my face are beyond description. Beyond forgetting.

BOSQUE DEL APACHE, FLY-IN

Today we watched our Sandhill Cranes from the convenience of a tall tower at the State Wildlife Refuge this side of Belen. We were alone, since most of the people were at the Bosque. The Cranes were foraging in the fields but when we stopped the car, all heads came up and all eyes followed our movements. We climbed the stairs up onto the tower and then the birds seemed to forget about us. What a great way to spend an afternoon!

But as evening approached, we decided to return to the new ponds just outside the Refuge. It seems that other folks had the same idea, but everyone is courteous and we all watch the skies for the returning Cranes. These ponds are just the right depth for Cranes to roost in (not by accident, but by the efforts of the Refuge personnel). Other birds have already set-tled in to spend the night: Pintails and Green-winged Teal, Mallard and Bufflehead.

Since it's November, few mosquitoes are about. No wind at the moment, and the shallow water reflects the tawny desert hills. The sky grows to a darker blue and a small cloud is lined with silvery-gold backlighting from the setting sun. And here they come...a flock of twenty or so...winging in from the south. They aren't very high and they descend rapidly. Wing flaps drop...legs dangle and they paraglide. Touch down...a couple of running steps...the proverbial "piece of cake." Fluff the feathers, get a drink or take a quick bath, and then begin foraging along the muddy shores.

A serious photographer sets up equipment. Apparently the concern is the sunset, not the approaching line of Cranes. They come into their paraglide, astonishing one group of observers. Train the binoculars...wave on wave of Cranes come toward us. Line on line of Snow Geese come, but they seem to veer off toward the Bosque behind us. Listen...the indescribable, unforgettable sound of Cranes. Far away and distant, close at hand and loud.

The evening darkens and still they come. Against the turquoise blue of the desert sky, the luminous crescent moon drifts among wavering lines of Cranes and Snow Geese. Headlights come on. It's nighttime. Still they come...more quietly...more purposefully. All of the cars are gone. The sky above is filled with bright stars. Allen and I stand, watching, listening. No sound now but for the birds settling in to roost. Privileged are we.

It's Winter Time

Witchgrass
Panicum capillare

NORTHERN HARRIER

Low sun...cloud bank along the horizon...not much time before I lose the light. Strong wind...cold...nothing flying today. Not even a tiny bit of open water...the light-colored lines that I thought might be leads are only strips of clear ice. The sparkling spots are ice crystals upended. Not even a Mallard today...pressure ridges in the ice instead. Suddenly a low-flying raptor coming out of nowhere...only a few feet above the grass. Wings horizontal, tilting back and forth ...wingspan's well over 3-feet. There's the unmistakable white rump patch of the Northern Harrier. Dark brown above and tan beneath, so it's a female. I recall watching these birds "harry" small prey back and forth across this wetland until the final pounce. So "harrier" seems a better name to me than the general sounding "marsh hawk." Their primary diet is mice  and such but, like all birds of prey, they'll take anything that they can get, including carrion and other birds...the European name of "Hen Harrier" seems a bit farfetched...the bird's not really that big. Now she goes hedge-hopping over the line of brush...hovering into the wind...wings tilted upward ...now blown by the wind, makes a steep banking down just barely above the marsh grass. A sharp turn, across the road with little to spare. A couple of years ago I consistently saw a pair, the brown female and the gray male, just north of the east ponds. The summer breeding range for these birds extends to the tip of Alaska with the wintering grounds into

South America, but many are resident within the United States, and mated pairs occur in our region. I've never seen the twenty-five foot, U-shaped courtship dive of the male, the midair food exchange, or any fledglings. Maybe next season. Now she's working across the pasture...back over the downed tules. Can't make out much of her face...the facial feathers are supposed to be similar to those of an owl, enabling her to hunt by sound as well as by sight. Now back and forth across the lee side of the Dobe slope with its shadscale and cactus...up and gone down the valley. Considering the Harrier's expenditure of energy and her small prey, she lives on a very thin edge of existence, indeed.

EAGLE ON ICE

Blustery this February afternoon. I guess that our "false spring" is about over. Drive over to the dam to check on the ice...nearly solid except for the shallow edges. I must remember to check the journal for ice-out dates. There are a dozen or so Mallards on the other side in the flooded cottonwood grove. But no other birds.

Now drive over to Crane Point. There's some open water along the shorelines and in the wetlands to the north of the road. Mallards again, Canada Geese...one lone Great Blue Heron. Scan the bits of open water...wind's picking up now, quite choppy...but there are some birds out there...sitting low in the water...typical of Common Mergansers. A large group with whitish breasts and gray bodies... females? But against the far shore...bright white bodies and dark heads...males. There must be over a hundred all together. They are often the first arriving migrants and seeing them means "spring's on the way." But out where the inlet flow meets the main body of ice...two large birds. Eagles?

Over the causeway to the eastern end where my view will be better. Two adult Bald Eagles. I wonder if they're the same ones that frequent the north inlet trees...magnificent birds. At one time these birds nested over most of North America, but habitat loss and persecution as "varmints" severely reduced their numbers. Because they are at the top of the food chain, they were greatly affected by pesticide poisoning. I've searched my childhood memories and haven't found a Bald Eagle there at all. Now they're protected and welcomed as regular winter visitors here at the Basin. To the naked eye they don't look very big, but I recall that they are a long way off. They're nearly a yard long with a wing span of over 6-feet and weigh about 9-pounds: a lot of bird!

Another big bird comes gliding down toward the other two. No distinctive white head or tail...just an overall mottled appearance...likely an immature Bald. The two adults seem to accept the newcomer. I always wonder why birds stand on the ice...seems like little food and less comfort to me. But now two more eagle-sized birds come over Antelope Hill...adult Balds...descending...landing near the others. Fluff and straighten the feathers and all five amiably stand around on the ice. Not feeding or preening...just standing. The immature is at the very edge of the ice...oops! But it isn't at all distressed as the ice gives way...wings spread, sort of fledgling flight...both feet down and through the ice again. Doesn't seem to be looking for food...repeat the procedure...a game?

There's another immature coming in from the east...where did he come from! And shadows above me now...two more birds right overhead...mottled dark plumage with whitish areas on the tail and the undersides of the wings. And these join the others...now there's a bit of agitation...finally accepted. Now all four immatures are at the ice edge...fledgling flight...feet out and down...bounce and up again. Repeated until the ice breaks beneath them. I suppose that the softening ice has a bit of give to it...a trampoline of sorts for Hart's Basin Eagles!

Sometimes these extraordinary birds of prey can be seen by the dozen where carrion is left out for them, but to see eight here with four adults and four immatures is unlikely to the extreme. Bounce...bounce...bounce and then flutter away. Back again, and again. The adult Eagles appear to stare off into the distance, seemingly to disdain or even notice such antics. From my human point of view, it looks like fun...if you're an Eagle.

AMERICAN KESTREL

As we cross the railroad tracks and turn onto Highway 92, here is my first Kestrel of the day, perched on the power line. Drive down two power poles farther and here is the second little raptor. These 9-inch-long birds have distinctive facial features, including two dark streaks (called whiskers) down the sides of the face. In addition, there's a red cap and a dark spot that looks like an ear. The back is a bright rust color while the streaked breast is quite light. The sexes are alike except the male's wings are a brilliant blue.

Stop in the pull-out at the next railway crossing...this female Kestrel watches warily, but I don't get out of the car, so she seems to accept our presence. Now I can see her rust-colored tail clearly...and there is the black barring, just as the field guide indicates. The male's reddish tail is unbarred...this feature isn't easily spotted, and I'm pleased to see the difference so clearly today.

On toward Delta and now we're adjacent to Leon's Farm. Here's a blue-winged male Kestrel...unbarred reddish tail...then another by Caja's Veggie Stand...two all rust-colored females across from Mesa View Mortuary. A goodly population to admire. Though they nest in our area, they make an altitudinal migration down from the high country when the weather is severe. Now they've staked out their valley territories for the winter's stay.

This colorful, Robin-sized raptor occurs throughout North and South America and has adapted to civilization. A cavity nester, it's choice is a hollow in a tree, perhaps an abandoned Flicker or Woodpecker hole, but reportedly it will nest on a cliff face or in a niche within a building. During courtship, the male circles above the perched female who repeatedly calls. Then the two cooperate in building the nest, although it's not much of a construction project, since there's usually little material added. They both tend the three or four young that fly within a month of hatching. If conditions are good, the pair may have a second brood, with the male feeding the fledglings as well as the incubating female. Keeps him busy.

The bird's basic diet ranges from crickets to carrion. In fact, it's known as a champion mouser and consumes insects, small mammals, and reptiles. A rapid flyer, it most frequently hunts from a perch such as these along this highway or from trees and handy poles. It will watch, spot the prey, and swoop down. Sometimes, rather than perching, Kestrels hover over fields and wetlands. The Hummingbirds are specially designed for such flight but, otherwise, hovering is uncommon in the bird world. If the winds are favorable, our Northern Harrier may occasionally hover over fields or marshes when it appears to "hang into the wind" (flying forward at a speed equal to that of the wind). A difficult task that the Kestrel practices frequently.

In the past, this small raptor was known as Sparrow Hawk from its resemblance to the European Sparrow Hawk, and it can take smaller birds in flight, but such hunting requires a great deal of energy. And the European Sparrow Hawk is a member of the Accipiter group with broad, short wings, represented on our continent by the Northern Goshawk, the Sharp-shinned, and Cooper's Hawk.

This smallest of our Falcons fits our vision of "falcon": a swift-flying, trim, and streamlined silhouette with narrow, pointed wings and long, slim tail. True Falcons (there are over thirty species worldwide) look and behave like "falcons." They are known to stoop: gaining altitude and then diving straight down with folded wings. This set of birds is probably best known by the Peregrine Falcon, which also occurs throughout Eurasia. But included are also our dark-colored Merlin at 10-inches, the brownish Prairie Falcon at 16-inches, and the northern-dwelling grayish Gyrfalcon at 22-inches.

Our bird is properly *Falco sparverius*. Latin "falco" refers to the sickle shape of the bird's talons and "sparverius" is Latin for the European Sparrow Hawks that are all actually Accipiters (seems a bit of a misnomer to me). Our Kestrels are with us all year, preferring open sites such as our fields and wetlands. Their colorful plumage and habit of perching make them easier to observe and identify than most other raptors. They can almost always be seen along this stretch of highway going into Delta, adding bits of color to our wintry landscape. They've certainly brightened this mundane shopping trip into Delta.

COMMON MERGANSER

From Crane Point I can see at least a hundred white birds out on the reservoir...most are along the northern edge of the ice. At the northeast end, where there is soggy vegetation, there are ducks beyond count. Canada Geese graze in the areas adjacent to the roadway, where I hope there will be some water when the Cranes begin to arrive this coming spring.

Down to the causeway for a better look. It's wonderful to have birds at Hart's Basin again but with the low water level, they're still a long way off...really need the spotting scope. Estimate over 900 Mallards in the wet grassy areas. A loud whir of wings and they all take off in panic flight. Check the sky and there's a raptor headed north up the valley...Red-tailed Hawk? So that's what a thousand ducks looks like in flight! Now they bank and begin to return but land instead along the "ice beach."

And there are the white-bodied birds...black heads and long, narrow red bills...Common Mergansers. Many are preening, a few bathing, and several appear to be dozing. There are more in the water...diving then reappearing...their primary diet is fish and there's a good supply of carp here. Magnification up and the black heads are actually a very dark green. I can make out the rough edges of the bills...the better to grip slippery fish. Some common names for these inland, fresh water Ducks are Sawbill and Fish Duck. The same species occurs in Europe where they're

known as Goosander and, at nearly 20-inches-long, they're large enough to be likened to a goose. The word "merganser" seemed a bit odd to me and I looked it up a few seasons ago: Latin mergus = diver and anser = goose, so now the name is easier to remember.

One of them has a fish...oops! Drops it...grabs it again...the fish looks as long as the bird's neck! The Merganser stretches his neck up...tries to maneuver the fish to swallow it head first. I don't think he can manage it. Drops it...grabs it again and the bird begins to swallow the fish. Gruesome for the fish but fascinating for me to watch. What a struggle! Finally nothing but the tail sticking out of the bird's bill. The neck is greatly distended. Gulp! Now he adjusts the body and fluffs the feathers. No problem!

These large Ducks with a yard-wide wing span are one of the first to arrive in the spring at Hart's Basin (excluding the resident Mallards, of course), and they're often the last to move on northward to their nesting grounds in Canada and Alaska. I've read that they nest in tree cavities...can't envision that. Seems the drake departs the scene when incubation begins, leaving all the parenting to the female. With most ducks the females come in shades of brown (leading to the saying "ABD" or Another Brown Duck). But the female Merganser is in a class by herself. The body is gray, the throat white, and the head a rusty red. And she has a shaggy crest...looks like a punk-rock hairdo to me.

In the spring, the Common Mergansers are early arrivals and any white-bodied bird on our reservoir is probably a Merganser. When they start to leave, the Western Grebes begin to arrive and some will stay to nest. So, my rule of thumb: Mergansers in late winter, Western Grebes in early spring. Seeing the Common Mergansers here at Hart's Basin means that spring really will arrive, in spite of the weatherman's forecast of the coming storm. What a pleasure to see the reservoir alive with birds. To watch the storm swirling across the West Elks, and to study the Mesa behind me with its changing shades of bluish white.

THE EURASIAN WIGEON
A RARE BIRD

So many Ducks...Pintails and Redheads, Mallards and Ring-necks. There are several swimming in circles...stirring up food from just beneath the water's surface...white body with a large rusty side patch...Shovelers. And fifty or so colorful Green-winged Teal...there's an all-reddish one...Cinnamon Teal.

While Inez admires the ducks, I'm searching for my rare bird, the Eurasian Wigeon. A couple of years back, David Galinat, my bird expert, mentioned that sometimes this infrequently seen Duck may be spotted among a flock of American Wigeon. And there are plenty of American Wigeons here tonight...a nearby pair...the female's the usual brown Duck, but the male has striking plumage. His body is brownish-pink...there's a white band just in front of the black tail area. Now my Wigeon turns toward me...perfect, there's the shining white band across the top of his head...moving closer now and the broad green band from the eye to the back of his head fairly glimmers in the rays of the setting sun.

Check the rest of the American Wigeons near shore...and here's my rare Eurasian Wigeon! His head stripe is more ivory than the shiny white of the American Wigeon's and there's no green eye band. The other afternoon at Crane Point, I met Robin Nicholoff, my friend from the Paonia area. He wondered if the Eurasian Wigeon occurs here. His description certainly fit that bird, so I went looking and was fortunate enough to find it that evening. And now, two days later, the rare Eurasian Wigeon is still here for me to admire. What good luck!

On checking my records, I found that I'd seen this Old World Duck in February of 1999. Though it's a regular visitor along the northeastern coasts of our continent, it's considered as "casual" inland: meaning that there are a few records each decade in an area but the bird should be watched for. But "rare" is defined as seldom seen, but occurring regularly. So my bird is "rarer than rare." And since 1999, I've investigated a bit further. For both the American and the Eurasian Wigeons, the genus or group label is Anas, which refers to the whole set of ducks that we considered to be "dabbling" or "puddle" ducks, such as the familiar Pintail and Mallard. From my old books and the new book on *Birds of Britain and Europe*, it seems that both Wigeons are ground nesters with the female building the nest, incubating the eight or so eggs, and tending the chicks, who are quickly able to swim and follow her. Aquatic insects, grasses, and grains are the primary diet and both species of Wigeon nest far to the north of their respective wintering areas.

My rare bird moves through the crowd of American Wigeons and comes into better view...the body is more rosy-brown than the gray pictured in the field guide...but a guide is only a guide. Most of the ducks are still busy feeding but it's getting hard to see them...light's been gone for some time now, but it's been a wonderful evening of "ducking" with my dear friend, Inez.

It's Spring Again

Magic birds were dancing in the mystic marsh. The grass swayed with them, and the shallow waters, and the earth fluttered under them. The earth was dancing with the cranes, and the low sun, and the wind and sky.

Marjorie Kinnan Rawlings
(1896-1953)

First Light

Too dark to see much...up to the pasture gate and turn around. Back to the reservoir and pull off in the widened area. Put the spotting scope on the window mount...hardly a breeze but I see lumps...birds? Watch...yes, some of the lumps are beginning to walk around. White spots moving on the water away from the shore...Mergansers? Other brownish lumps...Canada Geese? The light slowly increases...the gray lumps are Sandhill Cranes. A few

heads are up but most are tucked under wings. They stand on one leg, roosting in the water...makes it hard for predators to approach without creating a splash. Occasionally I see reflections, so I know that dawn is nearer and that my count time is rapidly passing. A car roars by, shattering my solitude. Try to estimate my birds in sets of ten...well over 700 birds this side of the inlet. Another 500 on the other side. Big flock! I'm cold but there's no time to turn on the heater...dawn is nearer and the birds are becoming active.

Now I see Cranes along Vela's shoreline...still as statues with ducks and geese drifting on the water's surface, asleep amongst the sleeping Cranes. Nice arrangement. Over 200

Sandhills. Something white...three...seven white geese. One of them rouses...stretches and flaps its white wings...black wingtips, so it's a Snow Goose...then it goes back to sleep. A rumbling sound...train? There's the whistle and the folk song sings in my mind, "You can hear the whistle blow a hundred mile." Well, thirty at least. There's a low spot on Vela's shore nearer the road...heads appearing...a few...lots! Another 200 Cranes walk stiff-legged out toward the main reservoir.

A cool, cool breeze and I yield. Up with the window and on with the heater. Total's almost 1,700 Sandhills, the largest flock so far this season. Several are displaying on the near shore...watch with the binoculars. Wings outstretched... leap...bow...leap again. Though I've seen this before, it never ceases to amaze. And each season I'm asked: Where did they rest before Hart's Basin was here? I have no answer...a marsh somewhere? But I recall Aldo Leopold's writing of these ancient birds. He wrote that they're not restricted to the present but rather belong to the wider reaches of evolutionary time...that when they return to a place, they "confer a peculiar distinction...a paleontological patent of nobility, won in the march of eons."

The mist begins to rise from the water's surface. Gray ghost Cranes preening, walking, awakening. I hear a truck shift gears on Highway 65 a mile away. A wedge of honking Canada Geese...right over the car...then gone toward Vela's fields. Several Cranes stretch the body...then neck up and forward in pre-flight stance. Some join...now more...through the mist in the shimmery light of dawn they follow the Geese. A profound sense of peace drifts over me with the flood of dawn's light. Another of my precious images of Hart's Basin.

LEWIS'S WOODPECKER

Woodpeckers. Birds whose strong claws and stiff tails enable them to climb tree trunks. They have sharp bills to extract insects and to excavate nesting holes or to drum territorial signals. As with many birds, nesting sites are solitary. Clues to field identification include an undulating flight (flap-flap-glide) and, in our region, patterned back and wings. ENTER LEWIS'S WOODPECKER.

WINTER. The usual crowd of "little guys" are busy feeding on the ground around the ornamental pear tree. Several Juncos...a dozen House Finches...lots of House Sparrows...four White-crowned Sparrows. Our dominant Lewis's Woodpecker swoops into the area, and all the little birds scramble into the close-by brush piles under our big cottonwoods. Lewis pecks around a bit and flies back into the cottonwood. The smaller birds venture out...one lands on top of the seed  feeder...here comes Lewis in his circular swoop, part of his territorial display. Now Scrub Jay appears in the pear tree...down to the ground to glean seeds...King Lewis descends and Jay hops behind the tree...around they go...Jay dives into the brush pile. King Lewis returns to the seed feeder, hanging by his toenails...then up into the cottonwood, tailoring the seeds he has gathered to fit the crevices in the bark. He hoards but we rarely see him eat.

SPRING. The usual crowd of "little guys" have a tough time feeding around the pear tree for King Lewis will tolerate no other birds in his area. They must slip in behind him, snatch a seed, and flit away between his circular swoops. This tree belongs to the Lewis's Woodpeckers. Counted eight this morning. In the foliage above, a Lewis takes food to a hole in the trunk...all the motions of feeding young. There are three such nest holes in this old cottonwood, although we never saw or heard much serious excavating. The dominant bird, King Lewis, does nothing but display and maintain the territory. Perhaps he has the night shift at brooding.

SUMMER. Counted six Lewis's Woodpeckers this evening. One lands on the rail fence...just sits there...no, it's

begging...looks just like the others but the head is all brown with no red at all on the face...a juvenile. An adult comes to it with a moth...gives it to the young one. Fun to watch. Swallows are hawking (taking insects on the wing). A Lewis overhead...out of the cottonwood to perch on a telephone wire. Woodpeckers aren't supposed to sit on wires! Then out to chase an insect with a steady, crow-like wing beat. Catches and eats a moth in flight.

AUTUMN. King Lewis taps seeds into the bark of the cottonwood. Another member of the colony tries to peck at a pear in the tree...not nearly as adept as the Starlings, but he manages a bite or two before the pear falls to the ground and into the King's domain. The King investigates the fallen fruit...nibbles...flies back into the cottonwood. The second bird never leaves the pear tree.

Rather than the usual patterned back and wings of woodpeckers, Lewis's Woodpeckers have a solid greenish-black back, wings, and head, plus a dark-red face and an unusual pinkish belly. They can be seen regularly in the Surface Creek Valley but are considered uncommon birds in most locations. Their habits are unusual: minimal nest excavation, communal nesting, hawking and hoarding on a regular basis, perching on wires, and territorial displays to the extreme. Other birds dare not enter: Flickers and Downy Woodpecker, Nuthatch and Titmouse. Any bird that "walks" on trees is not allowed. So Lewis's Woodpeckers can be rather discouraging to us at times. But even so, we consider ourselves to be most fortunate to have this colony of unusual woodpeckers in our big cottonwoods.

RAVEN

Sitting here at the computer with a cup of hot tea at hand, I'm enjoying the audio tape of the Native American Flute as I begin my column for the *Delta County Independent*. My research on Raven is nearly complete: pages more than I can include about this very common bird. In my mind's eye, I see a small flock drifting across the stormy sky above Hart's Basin...a pair in flight, playing along a ridge in the Nevada desert...a single bird eating carrion along a busy highway with a seemingly clumsy lift-off. But these birds rarely become carrion themselves. And in the tape, Carlos Nakai's haunting melodies are answered by Raven's call. Now my imaginary bird perches atop a Pinyon pine on the Uncompahgre Plateau and lifts gracefully to soar in the updrafts along the canyon wall.

Raven (properly referred to as the Common Raven) can be found throughout Africa, Eurasia, and North and Central America. It is glossy black, over 20-inches-long with a large, heavy, all-purpose bill. Though Crows can 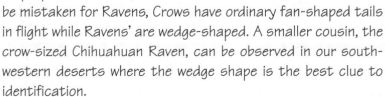 be mistaken for Ravens, Crows have ordinary fan-shaped tails in flight while Ravens' are wedge-shaped. A smaller cousin, the crow-sized Chihuahuan Raven, can be observed in our southwestern deserts where the wedge shape is the best clue to identification.

The Ravens' primary diet is carrion. This bird was known to accompany the buffalo, occurring continent wide. But now the bird is no longer in our Great Plains region. The noted ornithologist, Margaret Nice, believes that the Ravens' disappearance lies with the near extermination of the buffalo and the poisoning of the wolves: Ravens fed upon poisoned wolf carrion. And there is evidence that these birds followed the wolves or wolf tracks in expectation of feeding upon their kills. Of course, Raven is omnivorous and will take live food such as small mammals, various invertebrates, eggs, and young birds. This practice has led to an unsavory reputation, as it has with all members of the Corvid Family (Crows, Ravens, Jays, Magpies). These birds are large, noisy, and gregarious so that we notice them before we note such behavior in other birds, such as a Sandhill Crane raiding the Red-winged Blackbird's nest. But Raven also takes fruits and insects as well: Just about anything will do.

These winter residents of North America form long-term pair-bonds and both adults tend the young, which are slow in developing. About forty days are required before they can fly. They may be observed in pairs or in large flocks, and they may "mob" Eagles or Hawks and be "mobbed" themselves by smaller birds. Stewart James reported an unusual situation in Oregon. As his researchers climbed up to investigate a cliff-side Raven nest, the adult birds flew away. However, as the researchers later descended the cliff, the Ravens returned, and one of the birds picked up rocks in its beak and flipped them down the cliff at the humans. And locally, golfers tell of these birds stealing their golf balls. Their acrobatics in flight are as fascinating as any Eagle or Hawk: They climb high then tumble downward together or singly, and several will seemingly chase each other.

Raven plays many roles: Poe's "thing of evil," Noah's first scout, and a totem to the peoples of the Pacific Northwest. This bird's behaviors and its relationship to humans fills volumes. And Raven answers Nakai's Native American Flute.

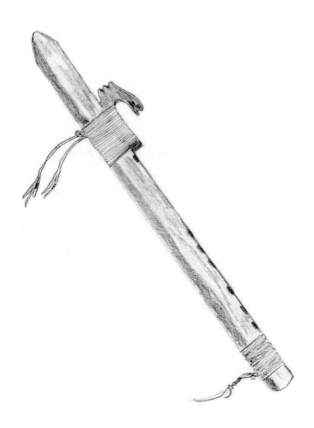

HOODED MERGANSER

Warm breeze...maybe spring is here? Or near? This evening's batch of Sandhill Cranes is foraging quietly along the northern shore. It's always such a privilege to watch them spiral down from the clouds high above. I counted about forty, but probably more will come in before dark.

Meanwhile there are lots of waterfowl to watch. Common Mergansers with their white bodies and dark heads are lined up along the ice beach. The usual marvelous gathering of ducks, all fascinating in plumage and behaviors. There's a whole group of the smaller Goldeneye...white bodies and dark heads with a bright white cheek patch that's much more visible than the bird's yellow eye. Displaying with that remarkable head-toss...stretch upright then throw back the head till it seems to touch the back...upright again...repeat the toss...stand on your tail and flap your wings. But wait...that one's not a Goldeneye! About the same size but the body is dark, breast is white, and there's a large white patch on the dark, almost triangular-shaped head. Moving around very rapidly among the Goldeneyes...hard to keep it in the field of view...lost it.

Here it is...magnification up. The white head patch seems to flash. There's a very small, thin bill...plain gray...it looks as if it were pasted on as an afterthought...seems unnatural. The white patch grows smaller...now larger as my bird charges toward a Goldeneye and the Goldeneye turns tail. As my bird pivots to pursue, there's a glimpse of black stripe between the white breast and the brownish body...the back is shiny black. No doubt, this little bird is definitely a male Hooded Merganser...and a female swims leisurely behind him. She's a small version of the female Common Merganser...has the same gray body and fuzzy reddish crest. The

Hooded is about 18-inches-long compared to the 2-foot-long Common Merganser. According to the field guide, my bird winters along the coasts of the north-west, the east, and the south-east. The summer breeding range is north into Canada and Alaska. Not even an indication of migration in our region but Mary Taylor Gray includes this elegant little Duck in her *Colorado Birds*. In one field guide, the bird's not supposed to be here, but it's included in another guide and here it is...another reminder that a field guide is just that, a guide, not gospel.

The diving, fish-eating Mergansers build their nests in cav-ities several feet off the ground...tough being a baby Merganser when it's time to leave the nest! I remember being surprised to read that the Mergansers and several other ducks are para-sitic: They lay their eggs in other ducks' nests, just as do the Cowbirds. Since the male Merganser has deserted and the female is alone, she must leave the nest to feed. In her absence, other hens may lay eggs in her nest so that she might have a huge brood to tend.

After seeing this handsome little Duck last year, I went home and checked out the meaning of the scientific name. *Lophodytes cucullatus*: "lopho" is Greek for crest, "dytes" for diver, plus Latin "cucullatus" for hood. But my Hooded Mergansers and the Golden-eyes return to feeding and preening and loafing. Show's over. Seems that my privileged moment has passed.

SEPT. 2002 HART'S BASIN WHOOPERS ARE GONE

The "green" reservoir stretches across my view from Crane Point...weeds have replaced the water and there's only a puddle left at the base of the dam. And what will it be like next spring when our Sandhill Cranes come from the San Luis Valley looking for a night's rest here at Hart's Basin? The fields below are dry, barren...no cattle. No corn, no oats or barley, so no silage and no waste grains for next spring's foraging birds. No income for the ranchers or farmers or orchardists. Drought is an ugly word.

And in the midst of my sad revelry, a recent e-mail floods into my mind. "The last remaining Whooping Crane in the Rocky Mountain Population has been declared a mortality by the U.S. Fish & Wildlife Service, marking the end of the bi-annual migration on and near the Monte Vista National Wildlife Refuge in the San Luis Valley." Kelli Stone, biologist at the Refuge, went on to state that the 19-year old Whooper left the wintering grounds in New Mexico in early March of 2002 but was not seen in the San Luis Valley and did not appear on its summering grounds at Red Rocks Lake in Montana. And so, Tom Stein (Whooping Crane Coordinator, U.S. Fish & Wildlife Service) has declared the death of "our" last Whooper.

But in my mind's eye, I can see a Whooper among the Sandhills as they spiral skyward against cloudless blue...and

again against the turbulent gray of storm. They're prominent with their gleaming white plumage and 7-foot wingspan until they're barely visible high, high above...heading for the Grand Mesa. Do I really see them, or is the flock only my wishful thinking? But I recall them landing in the evening and all the excitement...phone calls by enthralled Crane-lovers...watching the birds spiral down. I can still see them foraging with the Sandhills through Vela's pasture and down by the water's edge. And at the Bosque from the crowded observation deck...looking across a cornfield into a wetland area. The notice at the Visitors' center was accurate for here we find Kent Clegg's Whooper near the Willow Deck. What wonderful moments Martha and I have, studying this special bird with binoculars and spotting scope. For it was among those that followed Kent's ultralight plane from Idaho to the Bosque. And, as we prepare to leave, the bird calls. The sound is unforgettable, indescribable! Though I've several books with thrilling photos, and listened to this bird's call on tape and on video, nothing can compare to those sights and sounds in my mind's eye, for they are of my own experience.

I saw these magnificent birds here at home and at the Bosque and talked with Kent Clegg, who led the flock of

Sandhills and Whooping Cranes with his ultralight plane from his ranch in Idaho to the Bosque. When Allen and I first came to this area, I learned about the Cranes from Melvin Peterson of Eckert, who was the monitor of our Rocky Mountain Flock at their stopover at Hart's Basin. When Melvin retired, he and Rod Drewien, biologist, asked me to be the volunteer monitor of our Flock. And now my new toy, the computer, opens the doors to the International Crane Foundation, the North American Crane Working Group, Operation Migration, and no doubt many unexplored contacts. It's accurate to say that I'm hooked on Cranes. But the Whoopers are gone from Hart's Basin.

However, hope springs eternal. A number of concerned groups joined together to form the "Eastern Partnership" with the goal of establishing a migratory flock of Whoopers. Joe Duff and his colleagues have now guided Whoopers from Wisconsin to Florida with five of the first eight birds returning to Wisconsin on their own. There's now hope that larger groups of Whoopers will be able to follow this new ultralight-guided eastern migration route. And Florida's non-migrating flock is increasing. The captive breeding flocks are also growing.

So now my "innocent pursuit" leads me to contemplate a trip to Aransas National Wildlife Refuge or to the International Crane Foundation's headquarters in Wisconsin to see my Whooping Cranes again. But I revel in my good fortune to have known these ancient, magnificent birds while they were here at Hart's Basin.

NONE OTHERWISE THAN CRANES
'MONGST CLOUDS TOGETHER FLY
DIVIDING AIR WITH WINGS
AND ECHOING CRY FOR CRY

And as the maker of this anonymous medieval verse waited for his Cranes, so wait I. A few often appear in early March and, by mid-month, the large groups begin to arrive. We hear their singular cry so far above that we wonder if it's only our wishful thinking. Then, sometimes, we see the incredible downward spiral, as black specks above the clouds become great gray birds landing at Hart's Basin. But sometimes they fail to appear: Did they travel on, or was it truly our wishful thinking?

Now, I stand here at Crane Point in the first days of March. This is a year of continuing drought. Nothing to forage in the barren pastureland and fields below this hill, and I wonder what the birds will find to eat...only a few scraggly, weedy mustards are to be seen. But I know, too, that these ancient birds are hardy beyond our human conception. Biologists have told me of them roosting in freezing weather: Large groups standing in the water, with the birds on the outer edges sporting ice ringlets around their legs. I've seen them snow bound for days, striving to take off into the blizzard only to be tossed and thrown by the wind. To recall Steve Grooms' Cry of the Sandhill Crane, these birds were ancient before the glaciers existed, they soared above when the current Rocky Mountains were forming, before the rivers flowed as they do today. And a fossil Sandhill wing bone found in the Nebraskan deposits dates at nine million years. The drought that so impresses me is likely to have little impact on the Sandhill's view of time or hardships.

The predicted storm has arrived...spittering rain and cold wind. Only the lower slopes of the Grand Mesa are visible and the West Elks have vanished in swirling clouds of the snow that we all hoped for. There is ice on the shallow upper reaches of Hart's Basin as well as on the deeper water near the dam itself. But in between there is plenty of open water, and it's filled with this year's migrating ducks: Mallard and Pintail, Ring-neck and Goldeneye, Merganser and Teal. In years past, with more water, this springtime show could be viewed from the causeway, but not this year. Now the ducks are there, but distant, almost beyond my skills or my spotting scope's range. But I am grateful that there is water for them and for the Cranes that will soon be coming. I revel in the anticipation.

Scan the sky. Listen and wait. Only the sound of wind and the fitful fall of rain. So, for now, I must rely on my memory file. And I remember gentle breezes coming from the southwest. The human voices discussed topics of daily life but were tense with anticipation as we quartered and studied the heavy clouds against a bright blue sky. Karen called, "I hear them...look...there...to the left of Antelope Hill...Cranes?", and all binoculars turned. I couldn't see any birds. But Dave Davison spotted them...descending...a small flock that came through the saddle of land between Cedar Mesa and Antelope Hill. Closer they came, and we could all see them. Cranes!

Maybe it was only a small group, but the thrill was just the same. One of awe and amazement.

The birds seemed to grow as they descended...about two dozen. They turned and glided to the right...were lost against the grays and browns of Antelope Hill...but then they appeared

again. They banked toward the Grand Mesa and continued on toward the east. Clearly visible...the landing gear went down...long stiff legs that dangled below the large, gray bodies. They cupped their wing tips and went into their paraglide...the descent appeared to be leisurely until I realized that they had glided the length of the reservoir. Banked again and flew into the wind...lower...lower...lower. Touch down. A few running steps. Then they stood, fluffing their feathers. These 4-foot-tall birds walked toward the water's edge. They drank and were finally still, at rest.

The next morning the small flock prepared to continue their migration. Again we watched the pre-flight stance...they stood on tip-toe, stretched the neck up and forward. A few running steps and they were airborne, spiraling up and up until they were beyond our vision above Grand Mesa.

But today the wind grows sharper and the rain-snow mix obscures the fields below...can hardly see the reservoir now. It's time to give up. But it won't be long before this day's remembrance of Cranes will become a reality, and I'll stand again in awe of these ancient birds.

THE END

APPENDIX A

Cranes of the World

WHAT'S SO SPECIAL ABOUT CRANES?

Those who have not seen our Cranes of Hart's Basin are some-times mystified at our excessive enthusiasm. So what's so special about Cranes? Well, they're big birds, often as tall as a human. And they are bipedal, like us. They're noisy and gregar-ious and seem to get along together (at least when we see them). They're long-lived for birds, often reaching twenty years of age in the wild.

And they dance. We humans have mimicked them since our earliest times, in Africa, the Orient, Australia, and the American Southwest. It's hard not to notice the Cranes.

The pairs are faithful to each other and people ask me if these birds "marry for life." A better way of viewing their rela-tionship is the biologist's interpretation: The birds form "long-term pair-bonds." They appear to have a "family life" as they care for their off-spring, teaching it survival skills for an entire year (a long time in the bird world). So we respect them because, in so many ways, they seem much like us. We place our human values upon their behavior and they become symbolic. Cranes represent long life, harmony, fidelity, courage, and strength. In many cultures they represent insight, love of peace, vigilance: In short, we place our noblest aspirations upon the Cranes.

These tall birds appear in legends and myths and are always kind, compassionate, and loving. Whole volumes are devoted to Crane myth, and their image may appear on

Japanese wedding kimonos, symbolizing hope for a human marriage that will be as the enduring as the relationship that we see in the Cranes. They inspire the best in humans who observe them. It follows that their scientific name of Grus (Latin for Crane) appears in modern words meaning the quality of harmony, of agreeing, or of coinciding: congruent, congruity, congruous, congruence.

And we now know that these birds are ancient. Fossil evidence goes back millions of years. They were soaring in the skies above the Woolly Mammoth and the Saber-toothed Tiger. They were here as the mountains rose from the plains and before the last glaciers grew to carve and sculpt the peaks. It's nearly impossible to think about Cranes without recalling the famous words of Aldo Leopold: "...the other members of the fauna in which he originated are long since entombed within the hills. When we hear his call we hear no mere bird. He is a symbol of our untamable past."

And thus, my love affair with the Cranes. I was overwhelmed when I realized that there are Cranes all over the world! But obviously the place to start is in North America. Then on to Africa, Eurasia, the Far East, and finally to Australia. What a happy journey!

CRANES OF THE WESTERN HEMISPHERE: MIGRATORY SANDHILL POPULATIONS

Our migratory Cranes also fall into three groups. First, of course, are the Lesser Sandhills of Nebraska fame, the group that is best known. These Cranes, *Grus canadensis canadensis*, were called the "little brown Cranes," but they're hardly "little" (almost 4-feet-tall) and they're primarily gray rather than brownish. All of our migrating subspecies become brownish when nesting, but these Cranes are the most often seen. They dip water onto their feathers and often the water carries iron oxide, so that the birds become brownish or reddish. The "why" of this behavior is little understood, with some saying it's a cooling mechanism (even in the far north, the long days of bright sunlight could make things a bit too warm). But others contend that it's a deliberate behavior aimed at camouflage.

These birds weigh 7 or 8-pounds compared to our Greaters at 12-pounds for males and 9-pounds for females. Lessers winter along the Texas Gulf Coast among a host of other birds, including Whooping Cranes. But the Lessers also winter at various other sites: New Mexico's Bitter Lake NWR, northwestern Texas' Muleshoe NWR, northern Mexico, and Bosque del Apache in New Mexico (these fly to Colorado's San Luis Valley but then turn east to join the huge flocks that migrate over Nebraska's Platte River). The Lessers are known for the great distances that they travel, two to three times that of other Cranes, with some flying 14,000 miles round-trip each season. They nest along the northern Canadian coasts, in Alaska, and even into Siberia. These famous birds number over 500,000, and seeing their migration stop along the Platte is a "must" for bird-watchers.

For centuries, Nebraska's Platte has afforded sustenance for thousands of birds during their migrations to the northern breeding grounds. Interestingly, there is no mention of this incredible phenomena in the annals of the westward-bound pioneers who stopped at the Platte. It seems that the people and the birds were on conflicting schedules. The birds had to leave by early April in order to reach their northern nesting sites just as the snows melted and the insects hatched (read bird food). But the people couldn't begin travel until the mud dried out! So, they simply missed each other.

But modern development has taken a sad toll on the river. The Platte is known as a "braided river:" shallow, with spring flooding carrying and rearranging both the shores and the river bottom. Cranes roost by standing in shallow water and the Platte's changing sand bars have been a crucial haven. Furthermore, the nutrients found in the adjoining wetlands are necessary to successful reproduction. The banks need to be barren with no encroaching vegetation to harbor predators. Current aerial photos show tree/shrub-lined banks, the result of human flood control. And the crucial sandbar-roosts are fewer and fewer: They are apparent only in photos taken when the cranes are roosting. The shrinking river forces all the birds (cranes, geese, ducks) into crowded quarters, perfect conditions for the rapid spread of avian diseases. The river's survival, and that of the myriad waterfowl, is at a crucial point. Water diversions for irrigation and urban development have taken nearly seventy percent of the river. This potential disaster is put into better light when we realize that fossils found here in Nebraska show the Sandhill Crane to be the oldest, still-living bird species: six or more million years.

In the second group of migratory Sandhills, the Canadian or *Grus canadensis rowani* (in honor of William Rowan), the birds are sized between the Lessers and the Greaters with males weighing about 9-pounds. They are differentiated from the other two subspecies only by careful measurements of the longest leg bone (the tibiotarsus) and the upper bill (the culmen). They've been recognized as a subspecies for only a few decades and some biologists are still questioning that ranking. Their numbers are guessed at about 54,000. Very little is known about them because they nest in desolate tundra, inhospitable to human development.

The third migratory group is our Greater Sandhill Crane, *Grus canadensis tabida*. In the 1920s, when our Cranes were declining in population, they were labeled "tabida" (translation, "wasting away"). They are the largest Sandhill with wingspans over 6-feet (12-pounds for males, 9 for females) and they're nearly 4-feet-tall. There are four major groups. Our greatest interest is, of course, our Rocky Mountain Population of about 20,000 birds that winter at the Bosque del Apache ninety miles south of Albuquerque, New Mexico. They are the "Cranes of Hart's Basin." They arrive at the Bosque in October and November, roosting in the shallow ponds (created for their usage) and feeding in the fields (again, developed and protected

for the benefit of the wildlife in and around the Refuge). In November the Bosque holds the Festival of the Cranes, one of the premier bird-watching events of the nation. Although I prefer non-people events, this festival is worth attending. There are guided tours on the refuge and elsewhere in the region. Special trips are arranged into areas often not open to the public: to the "Very Large Array" with its radio telescopes that explore the universe; to the ISIS facility in Socorro that deals with seismic events on our planet; to the Trinity Site (first atomic bomb testing). An opportunity to visit the Sevilleta NWR is especially interesting since it is usually closed to the public (except for scientific studies and education). Its special concern is the reintroduction of the Mexican Gray Wolf.

There are lectures and trips on botany, bats, butterflies, and even on hummingbird banding. Other sessions include bird behavior, migration, and identification (song birds, waterfowl, owls, and raptors). And, of course, there are sessions about

Cranes, both those of North America, and across the world. There are sessions concerning the human history of the area, both ancient and current: local ruins, stories and legends, plant usage, and archeoastronomy. There are many opportunities for artists and photographers, plus special music and cultural events. But for me the sessions labeled "fly-out" and "fly-in" were worth the whole trip. Since the Refuge personnel know which birds will leave or return to which roosting area, our guides bring the tours to the very best locations. An experience of a lifetime.

In late February, the Bosque Cranes respond to the reproductive urge and begin to leave the Bosque. They fly north to Colorado's San Luis Valley and remain for a few weeks at this "staging area," feeding and resting. In early March, the community joins with the Alamosa and Monte Vista NWR to present a Festival of the Cranes. But at this time, some of the Cranes have opted to continue their journey northward and we are waiting for them here at Hart's Basin. On any given day, a few or maybe a hundred will cross the mountains, often flying over the "low pass" at Cochetopa Pass (10,800'). They arrive in late afternoon at Hart's Basin where they roost for one night. Then the next morning they leave us. But on that morning, another group leaves the San Luis Valley to arrive here in the evening. And so it goes for several weeks. The observers in the San Luis can't always tell whether a morning's flight of Cranes is merely headed out to feed or whether they mean to keep going. In fact, the birds may not make that decision until they're already in flight.

Each evening brings watchers to Crane Point. Listening. Anticipating. Sometimes only a few, other times even thousands of Cranes appear. The largest single group to date was over 3,300. The total for a season, 16,000. Not bad for an irrigation facility! People ask, "When do the Cranes come?" And I respond that they come on "Crane-time." Which is to say that they come anytime in late afternoon until dark. I've even watched them appear after dark. They leave us when the thermal updrafts are sufficient to gain altitude to cross the Grand Mesa (again, at over 10,000 feet elevation). In bad weather they may try to take off only to be driven back to this haven for another night.

But there are other populations of Greater Sandhills. Historically they nested in the upper Midwest as well as in the West. In 1930 there were only an estimated 25 breeding pairs left in Wisconsin. A pathetic fact, so well described by Aldo Leopold in his "Marshland Elegy." But perhaps there is hope: Wisconsin now has hunting restrictions and wetland restoration. And, on the Internet, the International Crane Foundation's annual Midwest Crane Count, begun in 1976, tallied more than 13,000 Cranes in 2000. These birds belong to the Great Lakes Population, which nests in Minnesota, Michigan, Wisconsin, and southern Canada.

Most migrating Cranes leave their wintering grounds and fly north to staging areas where they rest and feed before continuing further to the nesting grounds. But this pattern has a surprising twist for the Great Lakes birds. After nesting, they fly south toward their wintering grounds but stop off for several weeks at the fall staging area in the Jasper-Pulaski Refuge, Indiana (September to December), with over 32,000 birds accounted for in 1992. But the Cranes also stage here in the spring (February through March), so they have a twice-staging situation. And this refuge is within an hour's drive of Chicago.

And our Greater Sandhills have a similar, but briefer, fall staging area in the San Luis Valley. Kelli Stone, biologist, tells me that our Cranes congregate there during October and stay for two or more weeks. It's an excellent time to view our birds without the crowds during festivals. A must-do trip this coming year.

I've watched the birds at the Bosque and in the San Luis Valley. I can tell the Lessers from the Greaters but only when the biologist is at my shoulder. So this thought has crossed my mind: How do the observers determine the numbers of the Great Lakes birds? I've found nothing in the literature about these Midwest Cranes being all Greaters. Perhaps there are some Lessers or even a few Canadians tossed in for good measure. I'm searching for research data to show who's who!

There are two other populations of Greater Sandhills. One is in northwestern Nevada, including the Ruby Marsh where we first saw Sandhill Cranes. Impressed then, more impressed now. These birds winter in southern California. The last group on our list nests in south-central Oregon and winters in central California. This group was the subject of an article in the January/February 2004 issue of *Wildbird* magazine. The article, by Elizabeth Rush, concerns the efforts of rancher Dayton Hyde to help this population of Greater Sandhills. Hyde's book, *Sandy: The Sandhill Crane Who Joined Our Family*, is now available in its second edition.

But now I've found that there are other festivals and small groups of Cranes here and there. Happily, this indicates more preservation of wetlands and concern for all the creatures therein. The Internet has been invaluable in keeping track of this growing body of information about Cranes.

WESTERN HEMISPHERE:
WHOOPING CRANE

Paul Johnsgard's *Crane Music* (1991) includes a brief history of this ancient North American bird. As the continent was explored and settled, the first known record came from South Carolina in 1722 with the English naturalist Mark Catsby, who named the new species *Grus americana alba* (Latin grus = crane, alba = white). Though these birds were probably never common (perhaps only 2,000 birds at the beginning of European settlement), their breeding range apparently extended across the entire continent. With the opening of the West after the Civil War, the habitat was progressively altered. In the late 1800s the birds were pursued by collectors and killed by market hunters. The last breeding site in the United States was in Iowa, 1890. The last North American breeding site, in Saskatchewan, was eliminated in 1922.

During this period, there was a wintering population along the southeast coast with nesting grounds obviously farther north. Aransas National Wildlife Refuge was established for their protection in 1937, but the birds continued to decline and in 1945 there were only nineteen left. A project to locate the breeding grounds began in 1948. This detective story is portrayed in J. J. McCoy's *The Hunt for the Whooping Cranes*. Are the Whoopers nesting in Saskatchewan? Or maybe in Alberta? The Northwest Territories? A glance at an ordinary map hints at

the magnitude of the search: Canadian water-fowl plane surveys
with a watchful eye for Whoopers, ground searches with swarms
of black flies, false starts, biologists lost in the wilderness and
the no-show helicopter, study of old sightings in dusty archives.
Drudgery and danger. And finally a stroke of luck. A wildfire just
inside the northwestern boundary of Wood Buffalo National Park
and a sharp-eyed helicopter pilot: success! A pair of Whoopers
had their nest among ponds and bogs (safe from fire as well as

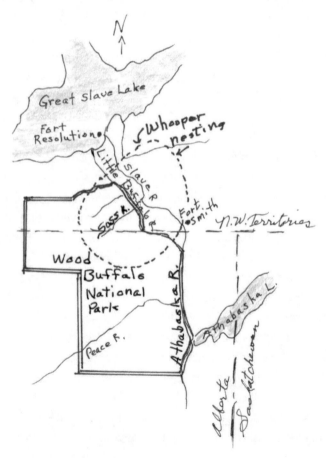

predators). On June 30, 1954, Bill Fuller (mammalogist with the Canadian Wildlife Service) returned to the site and photographed the pair from the air near the Sass River. Then more work, more search, and by 1955, the locations of the Whooping Cranes nests were established.

The Crane population slowly increased: twenty-eight birds at Aransas in 1955, forty-five by 1965, fifty-seven in 1957, and then the establishment of captive breeding flocks. However, all the eggs were in "one basket." With a hurricane, an oil spill, or an outbreak of disease, the Whoopers could suddenly become extinct. So in the 1970s the Canadian and U.S. governments began an experimental program to establish a second, independent migratory flock with a safer wintering ground and a shorter, less hazardous migration route of a mere 800 miles: from Grays Lake in Idaho to Bosque del Apache in New Mexico.

Since all Crane species lay two eggs per season and usually only one chick survives, single eggs were taken from the Canadian Whooping Crane nests and placed in the Sandhill Crane nests of the Grays Lake or Rocky Mountain Flock (now labeled Rocky Mountain Population or RMP). It sounds so easy! Until you look at an angry Sandhill Crane! These were the Whoopers that rested at Hart's Basin. Though their numbers reached thirty-five birds in 1985, they failed to reproduce, and in 1989 the project was abandoned with only thirteen Whoopers left within this Sandhill flock. Over the years since, I've watched their numbers dwindle.

In recent years, Kent Clegg and his associates have worked to develop better techniques for preparing the Whooping Cranes for life in the wild. The most dramatic part of their efforts has been centered upon teaching the young birds the migration route from the area of Grays Lake, Idaho, to Bosque del Apache National Wildlife Refuge in New Mexico. Martha and I were privileged to talk with Kent and to attend his slide presentation at the Bosque and at Grand Junction, Colorado. The young birds were able to migrate successfully and to live within our Rocky Mountain Flock of Sandhills. Although the two remaining youngsters chose to travel to our west instead of through Hart's Basin, there is reason for hope in preserving the beautiful endangered Whooping Crane.

Currently the reintroduction efforts have been concentrated in our eastern states. This second migratory population will winter in Florida and nest in Wisconsin. The plan is that these birds do not see humans: All personnel are costumed to resemble Whooping Cranes so that the birds do not imprint on humans. They are raised in captivity but then trained to follow ultralight planes. Sixteen yearling birds composed the "class of 2002." Another sixteen are in flight school, class 2003, and will migrate to Florida this winter. New information on this exciting endeavor is available on Operation Migration's web site (www.operationmigration.org).

And a non-migratory flock is being established in Florida. This 2002 season, for the first time in the last sixty years, a chick fledged in the United States. Name: Lucky. And he's doing quite well, thank you.

Information from the International Crane Foundation (ICF) located at Baraboo, Wisconsin, indicates that the Aransas flock now numbers 183 birds: a hopeful increase from the nineteen of 1945. In addition there are over fifty Whoopers in the non-migratory Florida flock plus over a hundred in breeding programs and captive flocks. Thus the world's total of these extraordinary birds now stands at about 400.

CRANES OF THE WORLD: AFRICA

GRAY CROWNED

With a crown of glistening golden feathers, how could any bird be but glamorous? Long ago, on one of my first Audubon trips, my fellow bird-watchers were in a frenzy because a Crowned Crane had been seen in our small nature park near Las Vegas, Nevada. Though it sounded exciting, I was amazed to see stolid gentlemen racing across the lawn and through weedy patches, tripods and scopes thrown over their shoulders. Now I understand. The bird, of course, had escaped from a private collection of exotic birds. But it was a beautiful creature and I'll always remember it.

The Crowned Cranes' natural home is in Africa. This is near-tropical habitat and these birds show some unusual characteristics. First off, they have four toes: three forward plus a grasping hind toe called a "hallux," so that they can roost in trees. All other Cranes have only three toes with the fourth a mere vestige and they can't sit in trees (at least not very well!).

Secondly, Crowned Cranes lack the trachea or elongated windpipe of the dominant Crane group referred to as *Grus* (which includes our Sandhills). So a Crowned Cranes' call is more of a honk or quack than the very familiar strong warbling of our Sandhills. The theory holds that the Crowned Cranes are a remnant of a more primitive group that was displaced by *Grus*. Thus it is considered to be the world's most beautiful living fossil.

The photos that I've found of Crowned Cranes at roost in trees are somehow amusing: To me, Cranes don't belong in trees! But they were still very pretty. Obviously native costumes would portray the plumage and dances would mimic these Cranes. It begins with head bobbing followed by bows and leaps. It must be very impressive!

There are two species, or is that subspecies? The world's Cranes may be viewed as fourteen or fifteen species depending upon whether the Crowned Cranes are considered to be two species (so fifteen) or as only one species with two subspecies (so fourteen). After reading about them, I accept the two species formula, for now.

The Gray Crowned Crane is *Balearica regulorum* (for the Balearic Islands in the Mediterranean Sea, plus "regulorum," meaning "of royalty," because of its gorgeous plumage). It

ranges across southeast Africa through Kenya, South Africa, Zambia, and Namibia. As the national bird of Uganda, it's regarded as sacred or symbolic. This has provided some degree of protection. Although it's the most abundant Crane in Africa, numbering about 100,000 birds ten years ago, the current population is down to about 85,000.

The bill is rather short and stout, the body basically gray, and the eye is light-colored. The top of the head and under the chin is black, but there's a bright-white cheek patch. The face is trimmed with red, including what looks like a wattle. But instead, the small sack-like structure can be inflated and is more properly termed a "gular sac" that can increase the resonance of the bird's call.

Although they roost in trees, these Cranes nest on the ground. They will not nest if their structure can be seen, so wetland drainage and overgrazing are major threats. Since they eat a wide range of foods and are more tolerant of humans than most Cranes, they're considered "generalists." These stunning 8-pound birds live in open grasslands, staying fairly close to water. They're not migratory, so if conditions degenerate, as with drought, they've really no place to go and may be seriously impacted.

BLACK CROWNED

This African bird looks much like a Gray Crowned Crane but is, of course, of darker plumage, so the golden crown seems more dramatic. This bird's scientific name is *Balearica pavonina*, meaning colorful (like a Peacock's tail). The cheek patch of the Black Crowned is red and white, while the Gray Crowned's is plain white. A field characteristic that I'd surely miss!

As is often the case, geographic location is the best clue to identification. The Gray Crowneds are found in southeastern Africa while the Black Crowneds occur in the transition zone between the Sahara Desert (on the north) and the more moist regions to the south. Within this transition zone, the African Sahel, there is an estimated population of 55,000 Black Crowneds, but in West Africa, the population is rapidly declining, with only an estimated 11,000 birds remaining.

The Black Crowned Cranes are non-migratory. However, their breeding grounds are in temporary wetlands during the rainy season and then they spend the dry season in large, permanent wetlands.

THE WATTLED CRANE

There's no mistaking this Crane. It weighs about 18 pounds (compared to our Greater Sandhill at 12 pounds). And it's the only Crane with a wattle. And so the question, "why a wattle?" Answer: Nobody knows for sure. But the wattle elongates when the bird becomes aggressive (as does the red crown of our Sandhills) and the wattle lessens when the bird is afraid or submissive. The call is high-pitched and rather screechy, but the bird is usually quiet since it doesn't often associate with other Cranes.

The body is gray, the neck white, and the bare crown is feathered (in contrast to our Sandhills). The face is red and the feathered wattle whitish. And it appears to have a long tail. But there is only a little tail, and what is noticed is actually elongated inner wing feathers (tertials) just as in our Sandhill Crane's "bustle."

The Wattled Crane is found in south-central Africa with smaller populations in Ethiopia, South Africa, and in the Zambezi Delta on Africa's east coast. It prefers wetlands along major river systems. So, a new danger for these birds: dams. The water is then controlled for human use and the habitat is altered both above and below the dam. The birds' feeding and nesting areas may become dry or, on the other hand, flooded. Since its favored food is sedge tubers and such, the food supply may be destroyed. Sometimes these birds seek food in fields and they may be poisoned by eating treated seed or sprayed plants.

Wattled Cranes can be aggressive and they require large territories, up to 250 acres. They fiercely guard their nests (consequently they don't attempt to camouflage it). They have the longest incubation (forty days) and fledging periods (100 days) of all Crane species. This is a long time to guard the young and, in addition, the birds often lay only one egg rather than the usual two of other species. And if two eggs are laid, the adults may abandon the nest before the second one hatches. So they have a very low reproductive rate. All of these problems have led to the bird's designation as the most endangered of Africa's Cranes.

Their proper label is *Bugeranus carunculatus*. The Greek term "bous" means ox and "geranos" means crane. The term "carunculatus" translates as a small piece of flesh, or a wattle. So, a wattled ox-crane. These birds are so large and so fierce that the name fits quite well.

THE BLUE CRANE

Again we meet a long-tailed Crane with the same sort of elongated inner wing feathers but here the "tail" reaches the ground. The upper head is white with a dark eye and the entire body a lovely blue-gray. Many Cranes show their aggression by enlarging the red patch on top of the head, but the Blue's crown is covered with whitish feathers. The bird controls these feathers and can raise or lower them (think of the crest on a Steller's Jay). But more interestingly, the Blue Crane puffs its cheeks so that it looks rather like a cobra's head. Hardly fearsome to us humans, but it seems effective enough for the Blue Crane.

The name, *Anthropoides paradisea*, is as lovely as the bird. The first part means "a woman" and the second part obviously refers to paradise. In clas- sical times, cranes were often associated with women because of the bird's graceful dancing, supposed piety, and intelli- gence. Blue Cranes often feed among springbok antelope in a symbiotic relationship: The birds help the antelope by being aware of predators, and  the antelope flush out insects for the birds to eat.

The bill is short and stout since this Crane consumes seeds and insects rather than probing into the ground, as do most other Crane species. The Blues are sometimes poi- soned accidentally or deliberately (for damaging crops). Occasionally they are trapped and kept as pets. They prefer grasslands, which leads to an interesting loss of habitat: The grasslands are being converted to tree plantations. The birds' numbers have fallen drastically: a ninety percent loss in the past ten years. But now there are groups concerned with this Crane's welfare.

This 12-pound Crane is the national bird of South Africa, which affords it some protection. But laws are difficult to enforce and may be ignored. Sometimes the birds nest beyond the designated sites, so that their protection may depend soley on individual land owners. Again, education and cooperation are the keys for its survival.

The Blue Cranes nest and feed in grasslands and their courtship is similar to that of other Cranes, with leaping and bowing. But mostly they run and run and run, with the female leading. Then they stop and call to each other and run some more. I can almost imagine that long tail flowing in the wind of their movement.

EURASIAN CRANES OF BROAD DISTRIBUTION

Frequently Cranes occur in limited geographic areas, but in the case of the Demoiselle and the Eurasian Crane, their breeding ranges cover vast regions of Europe and Asia.

THE DEMOISELLE

This Crane is the smallest of all Cranes, weighing only about 5-pounds. The scientific label is *Anthropoides virgo*, with the first part of the name meaning "woman"(just as was the case with the Blue Crane). The term "virgo" means "maiden" or "virgin." By tradition, the name was supposedly chosen by Marie Antoinette.

The Demoiselle is indeed beautiful. The body is basic crane-gray and the "tail" is long. The bill is short and the eye reddish. Most striking is the black neck, which culminates in long, drifting breast feathers like those we see in an egret. And a white line begins just behind the eye to become a long, delicate plume. Truly a lovely bird.

Their breeding range goes from eastern Europe across central Asia to eastern China. I've seen the term "Eurasian" many times, but now it has a good deal more meaning for me. The birds winter in Africa, Pakistan, and India. Of course they fly "south" to spend the winter, sometimes in flocks of 400 or more. So, some may have to fly through the Himalayan mountain passes, at 22,000 feet.

The dance of the Demoiselles is animated, quick, and graceful. Sometimes "audience" birds gather round to watch. Rather than in the usual wetlands, Demoiselles nest in uplands  or even desert regions if a water source is within 500 yards. Their nest is sometimes made of pebbles or, more frequently, the eggs are laid directly on the ground where patchy vegetation is tall enough to hide the nesting adult. And, of course, the nest, with its two eggs, is vigorously defended. The incubation period is about a month (the shortest of Cranes) and the fledging period is around two months (very short for Cranes). Many birds molt and become flightless during chick-raising time: Flying away from danger is not an option then. But not so for the these small Cranes. Their molt is gradual and they never become flightless. Johnsgard suggests that this may be an adaptation to dry land breeding, where there is no body of water that could harbor them from predators, and the only option may be to take flight.

The Demoiselles are the second most numerous Crane (next to our Lesser Sandhills of Nebraska). They are gregarious, adaptable, and their future is more secure than that of most Cranes. Their status provides some protection: They're revered in Islamic countries and a symbol of good luck in Mongolia and India. But habitat loss and pesticides are always threats. In Pakistan they are hunted with a weighted sling called a "soya."

Then some of the birds are released (to preserve the resource), while others are kept as pets: Considering the poverty level, I can't help but wonder what happens to some of the "pets." And the eggs would enhance a poor human diet.

Now that I've become a Crane-addict, I think that the Demoiselle is the Crane I most desire to see. It's unlikely that I could travel to Eurasia to see it, but there are captive Demoiselles at the International Crane Foundation's facility in Baraboo, Wisconsin. Maybe?

THE EURASIAN OR COMMON CRANE

America's Sandhills (500,000), then the Demoiselles (230,000), and then the Common Crane of Eurasia, *Grus grus* (200,000). The decisions in naming intrigue me, and this bird's name implies that it was the first to be described, or perhaps the most abundant, or the most important, or...

It ranges over 85 countries in Eurasia and Africa. It nests from Great Britain to Siberia. It winters in Spain, Egypt, Iran, Iraq, China, and India. It's most closely related to the Whooping Crane, but it looks more like our Sandhill: the usual gray body including the bare red crown and the bustle. But the neck is very dark, and there's a broad white stripe starting behind the eyes and extending down the nape or back of the neck. It looks rather like a racing stripe to me.

SD

These 12-pound birds have lost much habitat, especially in Europe (an estimated one-third of its wetlands have been drained), and the birds have all the usual problems as well:

pesticides, hunting, plus being overrun by human warfare. But bits of habitat are now being preserved, and in Germany volunteers are clearing marshes of brush and weedy growth to provide more nesting sites. The most charming bit that I've found in exploring the literature is that in the Scandinavian countries, the birds are protected and their annual return signals that winter (with its cold and darkness) is truly retreating. Near Hornborga in Sweden, local people set out potatoes for the Cranes to feast upon. In 1996, approximately 6,000 Cranes took advantage of the hand-out and over 120,000 people came to enjoy the Cranes.

ONE ANSWER GETS YOU TEN

One answer gets you ten questions. I have some answers about Sandhill Cranes and the Whoopers, and I've gained a bit of information about the Cranes of Africa. But what about the Australian Crane, the Brogla? It has a red crown that seems to have slipped backward a bit, so it appears to be more like a head scarf, sad looking but also rather humorous looking, too. It does not migrate. It's larger, weighing about 16-pounds. It sometime hybridizes with its near relative, the Sarus, that stands 6-feet-tall. And then there's the Black-necked Crane that nests in Tibet at 13,000 to 15,000 feet elevation. Little is known about its habits and it is currently being studied.

Australian Crane,
the Brogla
Grus rubicundus

Perhaps the most beautiful of all is the Japanese Crane. It is much like our Whooper, all white with a red crown and black wingtips. But the face and neck are black with a broad white line from the back of the eye down the nape of the neck. It's revered and symbolic of good fortune. But unfortunately, as is so often the case, we humans

Sarus Crane
Grus antigone

Red-crowned or
Japanese Crane
Grus japonensis

misuse and abuse that which we love. Habitat loss and human population pressure has led to this elegant 25-pound bird's classification as the second most endangerd Crane (after our Whooper).

Cranes nest in the north and winter in the south, migrating north-south. And the entire northern rim of the Eurasian continent with its long summer days and abundant insects (read: Crane chick food) harbors a whole set of Cranes. Among those nesting Cranes is the 9-pound Hooded Crane, labeled *Grus monacha*, with the species name meaning "hooded like a monk." The body is dark but the head and neck are white, hence "hooded."

Hooded Crane
Grus monacha

These birds prefer to nest in damp moors and in boggy larch forests that aren't easily studied. In fact, this Crane was first seen and then described in its summering areas. But the first nest wasn't found until 140 years later.

The White-naped Crane is a larger bird weighing about 13-pounds. As usual, the body is gray, but the back of the neck (the nape) is white. The face is red and there's a bit of white under the chin. They

White-naped
Crane
Grus vipio

nest in swampy or grassy areas, in forest steppe habitats or lake depressions. They winter in marshes, rice paddies, along mud flats, or sandbars in shallow lakes. Along with many other birds, the White-naped Cranes winter in the Demilitarized Zone of Korea. Of course, the situation there is very unstable and our Cranes could easily fall victim to human warfare.

Siberian Crane
*Bugerans
leucogeranus*

Finally there's the large 17-pound Siberian Crane. In flight they are lovely with their all-white bodies and black wingtips. Pictures of them remind me of Whoopers. But their red faces present a comical aspect. They are unique among Cranes, for they eat fish and have serrated bills. They nest in the extreme north and winter in Iran, China, and in India, where they're known as the "lily of birds." Although they're basically white, they're unrelated to any of the other white Cranes:

Black-necked
Crane
Grus nigricollis

Their closest relative seems to be the Wattled Crane of Africa (*Bugeranus carunculatus*). The Siberian Cranes nest in arctic tundra and in marshy areas within the northern taiga forests in Siberia. Their territories are large, often with the nests separated by several miles.

There's a book or seven on a library shelf somewhere about each of these birds. But I read recently that a sign of good mental health is a full "in-basket." So I guess I'm OK!

CRANES: WHO'S WHO & WHO'S WHERE NORTH AMERICA & THE WORLD

SANDHILL CRANE with six subspecies
(*Grus canadensis*) Latin "grus" means crane.
The symbol **"e"** indicates very endangered.

a. Cuban (*Grus canadensis nesiotes*)
Greek "nesiotes" = islander
size: less than 11 lbs.
location: limited to Cuba
e *numbers*: 54

b. Florida (*Grus canadensis pratensis*)
Latin "pratensis" = of the meadows
size: 11 lbs.
location: resident, primarily in Okefenokee Swamp
numbers: 245

c. Mississippi (*Grus canadensis pulla*)
Latin for "very dark"
size: similar to Florida
location: Jackson County, Mississippi
e *numbers*: 110-120

Notable as the first birds to force the rerouting of an interstate highway. Established as a separate subspecies (not just another group of Florida Cranes) by John Aldrich in 1997.

d. Lesser (*Grus canadensis canadensis*)

size: 4-feet, 7-8 lbs.

location: nests in northern Canada and even into Siberia. Winters along Gulf Coast of Texas, northern Mexico, New Mexico's Bitter Lake NWR & northwest Texas' Muleshoe NWR. Some winter at Bosque del Apache: In spring migration, they fly from the Bosque to the San Luis Valley but then turn east to join the huge flocks that migrate over Nebraska's Platte River.

numbers: 500,000

e. Canadian or intermediate (*Grus canadensis rowani*)

Named in honor of William Rowan.

size: between Greater & Lesser

location: nests in tundra regions of central Canada, winter on Gulf Coast, staging area at Nebraska's Platte River

numbers: estimated 54,000

f. Greater (*Grus canadensis tabida*)

Latin for "'wasting away.'" The population was dwindling in 1925. Much better now!

size: The largest subspecies at 4-feet-tall. Males at 12 lbs. and females at 9 lbs.

location: These are the Cranes that come to Hart's Basin (the Rocky Mountain Population, RMP). Recent research includes other populations throughout the West as well as the Great Lakes Population (GLP) with 31,600 and smaller groups in Oregon & California.

numbers: Our RMP numbers about 20,000

CRANES OF THE WORLD

EUROPE

Common or Eurasian Crane. Broad breeding range, 60,000 to 100,000. About 12 lbs. (Our Sandhill is also about 12 lbs.)

Demoiselle. Translates as "lovely lady." The smallest Crane at 5 lbs.

ASIA

Hooded. Nests in inaccessible regions of Siberia. About 9 lbs.

Siberian. All white with a red face. About 17 lbs.

(Our Whooper is also about 17 lbs.)

White-naped. Gray color. Found in Russia, Korea, China. 13 lbs.

Black-necked. Gray color. Nests in remote areas: the least-studied Crane. 12-14 lbs.

Japanese or Red-crowned. Majestic, much like our Whooper but weighs up to 25 lbs., the world's largest Crane.

AFRICA

Blue. Blue-gray body. If excited, puffs up its head (looking ratherlike a cobra). About 12 lbs.

Crowned. Glamorous with exotic golden crown. Two species. 8 lbs.

Wattled. Dark gray with whitish wattle dangling below bill. Fiercely territorial. 18 lbs.

FAR EAST AND AUSTRALIA

Sarus. Four flocks. Sacred in India. The tallest Crane at 6-feet.

Australian or Brogla. Blue-gray. About 16 lbs. (hybridizes with Sarus)

NOTE: The work of the International Crane Foundation (ICF) is the protection and preservation of all of the world's Cranes. www.savingcranes.org

EPILOG, WHOOPING CRANE
MARCH 2004

The Aransas Flock
Migration over 2,000 miles from the Gulf states to Buffalo Wood National Park in Canada. North American Crane Working Group indicates 173 birds.

Florida's Non-migratory Flock
First chick fledged in the past 60 years in the United States: male, name is "Lucky." In the spring of 2003 two more chicks fledged in the flock, so it now numbers over 100 birds.

A Second Migratory Flock
The effort to establish a second migratory flock in the eastern United States is going well. Migration route: Necedah NWR in Wisconsin to Chassahewitz NWR in Florida, 1,250 miles.

"Class of 2001" with 6 birds migrated on their own to the Florida wintering grounds: 4 survive

"Class of 2002" with 16 birds migrated with ultralight airplanes, from Wisconsin to Florida, fall of 2002

"Class or 2003" with 16 birds migrated with ultralight airplanes, again from Wisconsin to Florida, fall of 2003

GOAL: established flock of 223 birds, with 25 nesting pairs, by 2020

Captive Breeding Flocks

Calgary Zoo, Calgary, Canada

Patuxent Wildlife Research Center, Laurel, Maryland

San Antonio Zoo, San Antonio, Texas

Species Survival Center, Audubon Institute, New Orleans,
    Louisiana

TOTAL WORLD POPULATION OF WHOOPING CRANES NOW AT ABOUT 400

BIBLIOGRAPHY

BOOKS

Birds: a Celebration in Words and Paintings by Exley, Helen. ISBN: 1-85015-449-X

Bird Brains by Savage, Candace. ISBN: 0-87156-956-6

Birder's Handbook by Ehrlich, Paul; Dobkin, David S.; Wheye, Darryl. ISBN: 0-671-65989-8

Birds of Britain and Europe by Perrins, Christopher; editor: Attenborough, David. ISBN: 0-292-75532-5

Birds of the Great Basin by Ryser, Fred A. Jr. ISBN: 0-87417-080-X

Birds of Heaven by Peter Matthiessen; painting/drawings by Robert Bateman. ISBN: 0-374-19944-2

Birder's Dictionary by Cox, Randolph T. ISBN: 1-56044-423-1

Crane Music by Johnsgard, Paul A. ISBN: 1-56098-051-6

Cranes, the Noblest Flyers by Price, Alice Lindsay. ISBN: 1-888809-24-8

Dictionary of American Bird Names by Choate, Ernest A. ISBN 0-87645-117-2

Dictionary of Scientific Bird Names by Jobling, James A. ISBN 0-19-854634-3

Field Guide to Western Birds' Nests (a Peterson Field Guide) by Harrison, Hal. ISBN: 0-395-25629-2

Guide to Colorado Birds by Gray, Mary Taylor. ISBN: 1-56579-283-1

Golden Guide to the Birds of North America by Robbins, Bruun and Zim, illustrated by Singer. ISBN: 0-307-33656-5

Great Blue Heron by Allen, Haywood. ISBN: 1-55971-094-2

Hunt for the Whooping Cranes by McCoy, J. .J. ISBN: 0-8397-3500-6 (PBK.)

Legends of the Crane by Jensen, Pamela J. ISBN:0-9676879-0-X

Many Rivers to Cross by Montgomery, M. R. ISBN: 0-684-81829-9

Sand County Almanac by Leopold, Aldo. Oxford University Press. ISBN: 03-453-450-53

Seasons of the Crane by Stahlecker, Dale and Frentzel, Martin. Limited to Sandhills & Whoopers. ISBN: 0-910467-11-0

Sibley Guide to Birds by Sibley, David Allen. ISBN:0-679-45122-6

So Cranes May Dance by Katz, Barbara. International Crane Foundation. ISBN: 1-55652-171-5

100 Birds and How They Got Their Names by Wells, Diana. ISBN: 1-56512-281-X

Utah Flora by Welsh, S.L., Atwood, N. D., Goodrich, S., Higgins, L. C. ISBN 0-8425-2313-8

REFUGES

Alamosa/Monte Vista National Wildlife Refuge: Monte Vista Crane Committee, P. O. Box 585, Monte Vista, CO 81144; (719) 852-3552

Bosque del Apache: Friends of the Bosque, P. O. Box 340, San Antonio, NM 87832

Bosque del Apache National Wildlife Refuge: P. O. Box 743-C, Socorro, NM 87801

Lillian Annette Rowe Sanctuary, 44450 Elm Island Road, Gibbon, NE 69940; (308) 468-5282; rowe@nctc.net

ORGANIZATIONS

American Birding Association: P. O. Box 6599, Colorado Springs, CO 80934-6599; (800) 634-7736; www.american-birding.org.

Cornell Laboratory of Ornithology: 159 Sapsucker Woods Road, Ithaca, NY 14850; (607) 254-2473; http://www.birds.cornell.edu.

International Crane Foundation: E-11376 Shady Lane Road, P. O. Box 447, Baraboo, WI 53913-0447; (608) 356-9462; www.savingcranes.org

Operation Migration: Operation Migration-USA, P. O. Box 868, Buffalo, NY 14297; (905) 986-4384; opmig@durham.net [Whooper re-introduction]

National Audubon Society: 700 Broadway, New York, NY 10003; (212) 979-3000; www.audubon.org

Rocky Mountain Bird Observatory: William Palmer, 14500 Lark Bunting Lane, Brighton, CO 80603; (303) 659-4348; www.rmbo.org

INDEX

Alamosa, 110

Alp Lily, *Lloydia serotina*, 55

American Avocet,
    Recurvirostra americana,
    29, 114

American Kestrel,
    Falco sparverius, 127

Aransas NWR, 163

Aspen, *Populus tremuloides*, 96

American Pipit,
    Anthus rubescens, 53

American Wigeon, *see* Wigeon

Australian Crane,
    Grus rubicundus, 179, 185

Bald Eagle,
    Haliaeetus leucocephalus,
    124

Barn Swallow,
    Hirundo rustica, 47

Bindweed,
    Convolvulus arvensis, 25

Black-crowned Night-heron,
    Ncyticorax nycticorax, 32,
    110

Black-necked Crane,
    Grus nigricollis, 181, 184

Black-necked Stilt,
    Himantopos mexicanus, 32

Blue Crane,
    Anthropoides paradisea,
    172, 184

Blue Jay, *Cyanocitta cristata*,
    77

Bosque del Apache, 116, 157

Bosque del Apache, Fly-out,
    117

Bosque del Apache, Fly-in, 119

Bristlecone Pine,
    Pinus aristata, 94

Brogla Crane, *see* Australian

Bufflehead, *Bucephala albeola*,
    15

Bulrush, *see* Tule

Canada Goose,
    Branta canadensis, 18

Canadian Sandhill Crane,
    Grus rowani, 158, 183

Casmerodius alba, see Great Egret

Cattail, *Typha latifolia*, 60

Chamerion danielsii, see Fireweed

Cochetopa Pass, 92

Common Crane, *Grus grus*, 177, 184

Common Merganser, *Mergus merganser*, 130

Common Nighthawk, see Nighthawk

Common Raven, see Raven

Crawford, 85

Crowned Cranes, 168, 184
  Black Crowned, *Balearica pavonina*, 170, 184
  Gray Crowned, *Balearica regulorum*, 168

Cuban Sandhill Crane, *Grus nesiotes*, 182

Demoiselle Crane, *Anthropoides virgo*, 175, 184

Dipper, American, *Cinclus mexicanus*, 74

Douglas fir, *Pseudotsuga menziesii*, 95

Drewien, Rod, 148

Eared Grebe, *Podiceps nigricollis*, 26

Eastern Blue Jay, see Blue Jay

Eckert, vi, 6

Eurasian Crane, see Common Crane

Eurasian Wigeon, see Wigeon

Fireweed, *Epilobium angustifolium*, 43, 67

Florida Sandhill Crane, *Grus canadensis pratensis*, 182

Fruitgrowers Reservoir, v

Greasewood, *Sarcobatus vermiculatus*, 107

Great Blue Heron, *Ardea herodias*, 68

Golden Eagle, *Aquila chrysaetos*, 22

Great Egret, *Ardea alba*, 44

Great Lakes Population, 161

Greater Sandhill Crane, *Grus canadensis tabida*, 2, 5, 12, 21, 136, 149, 158, 162, 183

Hart's Basin, v

Hooded Crane, *Grus monachus*, 180, 184

Hooded Merganser,
    Lophodytes cucullatus, 144

Japanese Crane,
    Grus japonensis, 180, 184

Kestrel, see American Kestrel
Killdeer, Charadrius vociferus,
    37

Lanner, Ronald M., 94
Lesser Sandhill Crane,
    Grus canadensis
    canadensis, 156, 183
Lewis's Woodpecker,
    Melanerpes lewis, 138
Limber pine, Pinus flexilis, 96

Magpie, Black-billed,
    Pica hudsonia, 79
Mallard Duck,
    Anas platyrhynchos, 50
McCoy, J. J., 163
Merganser, Common, see
    Common Merganser
Merganser, Hooded, see
    Hooded Merganser
Mississippi Sandhill Crane,
    Grus canadensis pulla, 182
Monte Vista Refuge, 114

Needlerock, 87
Nighthawk, Chordeiles minor,
    88
Northern Harrier,
    Circus cyaneus, 122
Northern Rough-winged
    Swallow, Stelgidopteryx
    serripennis, 47

Pelican, American White,
    Pelicanus erythrorhynchos,
    57, 107
Peterson, Melvin, 148
Pipit, see American Pipit
Platte River, 157
Ponderosa pine,
    Pinus ponderosa, 95

Raven, Corvus corax, 141
Rawlins, Majorie Kinnan, 135
Red-crowned Crane, see
    Japanese Crane
Red-winged Blackbirds,
    Agelaius phoeniceus, 40
Rift Valley, 103
Rocky Mountain Iris,
    Iris missouriensis, 99
Russell Lakes, 84, 107

Saguache, 101
Sand Dunes, 104
San Luis Valley, 103

Sarus Crane, *Grus antigone*, 179, 185

Say's Phoebe, *Sayornis saya*, 97

Scripus pallidus, *see* Tule

Siberian Crane, *Bugeranus leucogeranus*, 181, 184

Sora, *Porzana carolina*, 59

Stein, Tom, 146

Steller's Jay, *Cyanocitta stelleri*, 71

Tree Swallow, *Tachycineta bicolor*, 47

Trees of the Great Basin, 94

Tule, *Scripus acutus*, 28

Violet-green Swallow, *Tachycineta thalassina*, 47

Water Pipit, *see* American Pipit

Wattled Crane, *Bugeranus carunculatus*, 171, 184

Western Grebe, *Aechmophorus occidentalis*, 62

White-naped Crane, *Grus vipio*, 180, 184

Whooping Crane, *Grus americana alba*, 9, 12, 146, 163, 186

Who's Who & Who's Where, North American Sandhills, 182

Wigeon, American, *Anus americana*, 133

Wigeon, Eurasian, *Anas penelope*, 133

Wild Iris, *see* Rocky Mountain Iris

Wilson's Phalarope, *Phalaropus tricolor*, 34

Wilson's Warbler, *Wilsonia pusilla*, 85

Witchgrass, *Panicum capillare*, 121

I hope you love birds too.
It is economical.
It saves going to heaven.

Emily Dickinson
(1830-1886)